Courtyard Housing

in Los Angeles

Courtyard Housing
in Los Angeles
A Typological Analysis

Stefanos
Polyzoides

Roger
Sherwood

James
Tice

Photography by
Julius
Shulman

University of California Press

Berkeley   Los Angeles   London

University of California Press
Berkeley and Los Angeles, California
University of California Press, Ltd.
London, England
Copyright © 1982 by The Regents of the
University of California

Library of Congress Cataloging in Publication Data

Polyzoides, Stephanos.
  Courtyard housing in Los Angeles.

  Includes bibliographical references and index.
  1. Courtyard houses—California—Los Angeles.
I. Sherwood, Roger. II. Tice, James, III. Shulman, Julius. IV. Title.
NA7238.L6P6   728'.09794'94   80-6057
ISBN 0-520-04251-4   AACR2

Printed in the United States of America
1 2 3 4 5 6 7 8 9

Photographs appearing on the following
pages were taken by Roger Sherwood:
p. 18, above left; p. 31, above left;
p. 33, above left; p. 35, opposite; p. 37,
below left; p. 37, below right; p. 40,
below left; p. 42, below left; p. 44, top,
above; p. 192, above left, above right;
p. 193, above left, above right;
pp. 196-197, left.

Photographs on the following pages
were taken by Stefanos Polyzoides:
p. 17, left; p. 21, below; p. 23, below
right, below left; p. 25; p. 27, bottom;
p. 29, below; p. 173, above; p. 188;
p. 212; p. 213; p. 214. Also p. 108,
Dr. Carlo Davis.

Contents

Preface

The unavoidable dilemma we faced in carrying out this study arose because we were not motivated merely by the desire to document and authenticate an era of building in Los Angeles. Certainly, establishing a public consciousness of the virtues of preserving a part of the exceptional building heritage of this city was a basic goal. Equally important was the search to find in the organizational and stylistic discipline of the courts architectural lessons relevant to the present.

Modern Architecture, the heroic international movement of the last sixty years, has left us in a state of philosophical ambivalence. The morally indignant frenzy of avant-garde prescience which characterized modern culture removed almost all our capacity to regard human experience as a historical continuum. The "new spirit" demanded that the future must necessarily arise from the ashes of the past. Consequently, the "enfants terribles" of Modern Architecture took a certain iconoclastic delight in propounding points of view that ridiculed traditional bourgeois and vernacular values and images. In the light of our immediate formal and philosophical precedents, we were expected to generate the brave new world rather than admiring or copying (the ultimate disgrace) the relics of the old one. We have also recently realized, however, that the old traditions are still with us and that they are as important as the dictates of Modern Architecture.

If Modern Architecture has left us in the lurch, perhaps some of its tenets need to be challenged. Is "alienation from tradition"[1] a necessary prerequisite to a modern point of view? What is really wrong with producing building forms and images that are coincident with popular and vernacular forms and images? Why should the use of precedent necessarily result in "the destruction of authenticity"? And how often is it reasonable to expect that the millennium should occur?[2]

The current rise of historicism is connected to the fact that the modern avant-garde standards of the 1900s have been accepted as establishment bourgeois values. The present mass preoccupation with nostalgia reflects popular concern that other substantial cultures have existed previously and are important to the resolution of contemporary problems. The diverse sojourns of our collective architectural memories have generated many and confused architectures, each claiming to be authentic and exclusive.

We live in a culture that is eclectic and, therefore, styleless. Populist nostalgia is manifest in the tendency to advertise the merits of a particular, partial architectural expression or to retreat through video images to a natural context long despoiled. As Modern Architecture reaches its nadir, the Marlboro Man slowly replaces the Modular Man as the dominant personality of the age.[3] And the style wars that characterize the everyday realities of Postmodernism are both inconclusive and destructive; the fundamental problems related to the making of places and objects relevant to human existence remain underattended.

At first glance, an analysis of some of the buildings of Hollywood's heyday may seem to be pure opportunism, a vehicle by which we may ride the popular crest of a nostalgic high. These buildings do seem to be implausible replacements for Modern Architecture. Just why, then, do we hold them out to be important models and prototypes? Our interest in the courts of Los Angeles rests in part with the obvious picturesque qualities of their particular Spanish Revival ambience—the tile roofs, the fragrant gardens and fountains, the incredible interiors, and those beautiful walls. What sane architect is not touched by these images? And we certainly feel no modern pangs of moral reproof because we love them so.

It is difficult to advocate the literal reproduction of buildings like these (although if it were physically possible, it would constitute a mere mild endorsement of Postmodern practices). Ways of life, skills, perceptions, and capabilities have changed in a manner that suggests it is still possible to ponder the design of special forms appropriate to our current situation.

The real value of the courtyard housing of Los Angeles lies beyond their obvious and seductive qualities. Our research focused not only on the recording of their physical character but also in the revelation of underlying principles that have been clouded by the doctrines of modern times.

The lessons of the courts have not led us to a pursuit of shallow, stylistic nostalgia by association or to a retreat from some of the unpleasant realities of modern life. Instead, they have helped clarify the shortcomings of stereotyped notions about architecture in general and the architecture of housing, in particular. Strategies about how to achieve a collective of dwellings in a dense urban situation without destroying personal amenities of individual dwelling and garden, concepts about communal living, and ideas about the relationship among the individual dwelling, the collectivity of dwellings, and the city itself all have potential for universal application.

The equal concern with organization in plan and section and with readability as expressed in an identifiable style in plan, section, and elevation is a methodological rediscovery that needs to be strengthened. The subtle weaving of places and things discovered with others remembered can become the basis for new architectural departures.

This volume represents a collective effort of almost four years. Our discovery of the courts began as separate experiences in the process of everyday living in this city. When we decided to combine our fates, we discovered that each of us had a favorite collection of special courts. Together we canvassed whole parts of the city, street by street, scoured Sanborn maps and aerial photographs. Courts were discovered singly or in great concentrations. We employed rumor, idle conversation, hunch, and blind luck as well as established procedures as the means of our research.

The significant examples of the court type in our collection were measured and drawn and were later photographed in detail. In the meantime, our plans for publication were being constantly upset by continual discovery. This present statement of our efforts is neither complete nor definitive. We have paused in order to record our thoughts and offer a number of issues for wider discussion. We intend that this book be used in part as a guide for the experience of some of the great buildings of southern California and also as a departure for the discovery of more courts. We hope only that the readers will help complete our efforts by contributing their insights.

Los Angeles, patio of El Coyote Café
February 1, 1979

[1] This is Renato Poggioli's phrase from *The Theory of the Avant-Garde* (Cambridge, Mass: Harvard University Press, 1968).
[2] We have paraphrased Colin Rowe's questions from the introduction to *Five Architects* (New York: Wittenborn, 1972).
[3] John McDermott coined this appropriate phrase.

Acknowledgments

We owe a debt of gratitude to the following individuals and organizations, whose help, support, and enthusiasm for our project made it possible.

Ms. Pat Ackos
Mr. Robert Bell
Mr. Robert McKim Bell
Mr. Michael Bohanan
Mr. Geoff Case
Mr. Edmund Dantez
Ms. Alice Mumper Davis
Mr. Carlo Davis
Ms. Penelope Ann Davis
Mr. Anthony DeFonte
Mr. Philip Field
Mr. Maury Grossman
Mr. George Hale
Mr. Raymond Hester
Mr. David Huntley
Ms. Lois Jolley
Mr. Howard Krieger
Ms. Frank Kuchenski
Ms. Idella Marx
Mr. and Mrs. Thomas Morris
Ms. Perry Osborne
Ms. Don Uhl
Mr. Kent Warner

Mr. Alson Clarke, Librarian, University of Southern California School of Architecture
Mr. William Cross, Pasadena Cultural Heritage Program
Mr. John Faber, Los Angeles County Assessor's Office
Mr. Alan Jutzi, The Huntington Library
Mr. Ralph Knowles, Professor of Architecture, University of Southern California School of Architecture
Mr. Thomas Owen, Los Angeles Public Library, California Collections
Mr. Baxter Ward, former Los Angeles County Supervisor, Fifth District
Mr. Felix Zuñiga, Los Angeles Department of Building and Safety, Conservation Bureau

The National Endowment for the Arts
The University of Southern California Department of Architecture Publications Fund

We would also like to acknowledge the contribution of countless colleagues and students whom we escorted through the marvelous buildings we examined and whose insights helped sharpen our sense of their true value to Architecture and to our city as a whole.

Introduction

1 The facts and principles that have shaped the urban structure, architecture, and landscape of southern California over the last century have not yet been fully established or explained. In view of the feverish pace of physical development that has so characterized the last 100 years of life there, it is no wonder that very few architects or critics have chosen to pause and involve themselves in introspection.

Of all available studies on the southern California environment, the great majority concentrate on the discussion of local monuments. If we consider typical architectural and art-historical preoccupations, this hardly appears surprising. Such studies concern themselves with the nature of individual buildings. They focus on assigning value to objects by establishing their pedigree on the basis of stylistic references to other locally, nationally, or internationally recognized monuments; occasionally they deal with the iconography or social history of buildings as responses to particular episodes in the region's past.

Recently, and especially in Europe, architects have rediscovered the polemical nature of common buildings. While common buildings are certainly of interest, it is important not to indulge merely in the analysis of the trite iconographic preoccupations of the common mind or to transform vernacular imagery into a new and contorted superconscious architecture, as the Venturis and their apologists have tried to do. Instead, the truly important issues of contextual responsibility and urban continuity need to be addressed.[1]

The word *type,* when applied to architecture, refers both to the images and to the organizational devices that embody the essential or salient characteristics of a certain set of forms. The ending *-logy* refers to the systematizing of the information inherent in building types into a doctrine or theory.[2]

The extraordinary aspect of typology as an operational device lies in the fact that it is generative. Two forms can belong to the same type but can appear and can be construed as different from each other. Therefore, a typological precedent does not necessarily lead to imitation but can rather lead to transformation. It does not necessarily bring about sterile

1

repetition of forms but can rather reinforce architectural attributes that are shared by many buildings at an urban scale.

Every city is a living reservoir of historically derived building types. Such types are formally consistent, stylistically diverse, and able to accommodate functional change. Such types are understood, not by reference to style, but rather in the degree to which they share common qualities, and also by their ability to aggregate some such shared qualities into unique places or elements that operate at the scale of the whole city. Typical examples of transformations from single common building to urban component are the street, the square, and the arcade.

The morphology of a city depends on the completeness-incompleteness or continuity-discontinuity of its typological structure. Throughout their history, American cities have experienced rapid growth, with the result that their typological makeup is extremely diverse. Typologies are generated or eradicated over time. At any point in time such cities exhibit a structure that resembles a mosaic of dated building types. City sectors can be seriously weakened by the negation of their historical typological composition. By contrast, the integration of new objects into an existing urban context can ensure the viability of both the new construct and the old city fabric.

The Los Angeles metropolis is a typologically super-discontinuous city because of its immense size (approximately 3,000 square miles) and the cultural pluralism that has dominated it since its beginning. It is therefore vital to insist on the preservation of traditional typological values in parts where such urban, building, and landscape order is either predominant or latent. Such parts become visible as crucial landmarks in an otherwise chaotic and confused conurbation. Also, the description, analysis, and design utilization of typological prototypes can intensify the process of providing order and identity to the isolated and heterogeneous urban components of this vast region.

Two serious mental habits stand in the way of a widespread acceptance of a typological emphasis in architectural history, design, and planning. Firstly, the disastrous vestiges of twentieth-century urbanism of ideological opposition to urban continuity and sociocultural specificity. The emphasis was on stylistic renovation at the expense of both broadly understood formal meanings and formal continuity. Secondly, our unique southern California culture is intensely weak when it comes to questions of collective memory or commonly held values. A condition of apathy or perhaps amnesia reigns when issues of the nature or utility of our cultural past arise. It should be clear that the pursuit of a typological approach requires reversal of powerful and prevalent states of mind among both creators and society at large.

If our decision to carry out a typological study can be explained as a rejection of past intellectual paradigms and the development of culturally relevant new ones, why are we focusing on the study of housing and especially on the examination of courtyard housing?

Of all common buildings that have relevance for the future of the form and life of the city, houses and housing are the most important by the sheer fact that they constitute the bulk of its building stock. Moreover, Los Angeles has always been an intensely private city, lacking in the physical presence of public institutions and the definition of an identifiable single public center. It is in houses and housing that our architectural life values are most clearly expressed.

A number of more prosaic factors also support the necessity to study housing typologies at this time. Southern California is experiencing a severe housing shortage. Not only is the existing housing the most expensive in the nation, but also there are not enough dwellings being constructed to accommodate housing needs in absolute numbers or by income. Land saturation is a recent reality in this region, and most new housing construction is carried out as second-generation building, replacing existing older structures. It is in this process that gross typological violations are committed. Many such trespasses are the result of exaggerated new densities applied to existing homogeneous low-density areas. Many others, though, are the result of ignorance, carelessness, or a typical lack of understanding of urban structure beyond the single building. The most common miscues have to do with the de-

Opposite
Figure/ground plan of the Echo Park area of Los Angeles. Notice the typological discontinuity of the city as it is manifested in the variety of sizes and shapes of buildings with a concomitant lack of spatial coherence.

struction of the street by loose placement of buildings inside their property limits; the complete inability to give the automobile as a source of movement or storage an appropriate architectural expression; and the development of living places that do not enhance life experiences and are not tailored to the particular qualities of their immediate site. In general, such new buildings are carried out without reference to the intelligent use of past models or the creative definition of possible typological transformations. They are destructive to the dweller because he or she is treated as a consumer and lethal to the city because they confuse its structure and its ultimate meaning. When people lose their emotional connection to the buildings they occupy, all architecture ends.

While the building of housing here proceeds at a slow pace—perhaps fortuitously—the process of overconstraining housing factors is intensified. Ostensibly for the protection of the dweller, national, state, and local governments have legislated a set of regulations or, more precisely, restrictions that make the development of a responsible housing form an almost impossible idea. Unreasonable building-to-open-space ratios, exaggerated dwelling-to-car-ratios, unnecessarily restrictive zoning, unreasonably high electrical, plumbing, and energy standards, bureaucratic control over structural safety, and deterministic access and fire-prevention requirements render housing design a mechanistic translation of banking recipes, building code formulas, and quantitative criteria into form. And they exclude most if not all valid historical housing prototypes that reflect respect for the city and the landscape and the life of the dweller. Finally, the inability of architectural factors to generate vital housing forms results in semantic triviality that is reflected in superficial styling. The imagery of new housing solutions lacks the meaning that is derived from either the memory of similar older objects or the excitement and anticipation of the use of homes as appropriate places for dwelling.

The need for an intense critical analysis of the housing situation in southern California at this time is unquestionable. We must discover and evaluate all our major housing prototypes in order to establish their utility and meaning in the present conditions of crisis of both conception and production. Of all the available housing types we isolated for study, the one that most captures the essence of a highly desirable but fast-disappearing southern California flavor is courtyard housing. The diverse examples of courtyard housing in this region are unique for two basic reasons: because they were generated in response to ideal as well as pragmatic demands about the nature of the house, housing, and the city; and because they also incorporated in their forms the force that has dominated most intellectual and practical activity here in the last 100 years—the ability to dream and to shape life and place out of a virtual physical and spiritual void.

California fantasies transformed into tangible realities have repeatedly shaken the world in the course of the century. Airplanes modified our measure of time; movies changed our visual perception; insurance and real estate innovations powered vast new economic changes; advertising altered consumer habits and world political processes; television restructured leisure patterns, social relationships, and personal sensibilities.

The Ideal of Mobility

The wish to move fast precedes the invention of devices that make fast motion possible. Early Californians became obsessed with locomotion possibly because it represented true freedom from the menacing huge expanses of western space and also because it represented an affront to conventional time-related experiences. The excitement of movement was expressed in the extensive acceptance and veneration of the car, the dirigible, and the airplane as cult objects of a new emerging world. The immediate formal translation of the ideal of mobility lies in the acknowledgment of the motorcar in the form of the city and in the forms of individual buildings. In their size and configuration, early Los Angeles streets are amazingly well adapted to the actual characteristics of cars and prohetic about the eventual effects of their widespread use. Courtyard housing in its developed typological examples accepted as early as 1923 the accommodation of the car within the building envelope. In both operational and expressive terms, cars as the embodiment of the ideal of mobility became important definers of Los Angeles urban order and building form.

4

Above
A Sunday outing in Los Angeles,
circa 1910. Angelenos were
obsessed with mobility from the
earliest times. (Courtesy of the
Huntington Library, San Marino, Ca.,
Whittington Collection.)

The Ideal of Instant Place

The original desert ecology of the Los Angeles basin was the cause of the inhospitality, landscape homogeneity, and placelessness of the region. In analogical terms, the urban structure of Los Angeles was also developed as a desert covering vast and undifferentiated private-urban-use expanses interrupted only by occasional places of commercial or public activity strung along linear movement routes. The ideal of place in Los Angeles is achieved by the exclusion of the surrounding context and by the definition of a protected interior realm that nurtures and safeguards private or limited shared values. Such places exude a sense of relaxation, respite, and perhaps even forbidden pleasure, not unlike the archetypical lifesaving oasis. The court as a microcosm becomes expressive of the idea of residential stability and order within a generally fragile social and physical frontier environment. The idea of enclosure becomes instrumental in the negation of exterior disorder and in the definition of the courtyard as a tool of collective identity.

The Ideal of Instant Culture

The vast spaces and the crushing cultural vacuum of the West demanded ingenuous architectural solutions whose civilizing influences were immediate and whose effect on the city was visible. The single-family house, as it floated in a continuous flat or undulating landscape between the mountains and the ocean, seemed incapable of defining community in form. In the urban areas where courts constituted a dominant and visible component of urban structure, the city incorporated an orderly hierarchy of public space. Streets, courtyards, alleys, garages were all afforded an appropriate architectural expression; at the time that they were actually created, they were used as bold urban-ordering devices in a landscape that was lacking in definition.

Whether viewed as space, building, or landscape, courtyard housing provided both concrete and symbolic references to the idea of a shared life motivated by concerns higher than the pursuit of mere survival. Whether through stylistic references or typological borrowing at a large scale, courts suggested the essential cultural continuity between southern California, located at the western edge of the Western world, and its European roots; and they allowed the creation of a city of familiar experiences that smoothed the life transitions of migrants and made their integration into the world of Anglo-Saxon values complete.

The Ideal of Entertainment

The distance from established eastern and midwestern centers of culture forced an early loosening of California morals. The possibility of novel behaviors and new ways of life has been a reality here from the beginning. As in all beginnings, though, the realities have been exaggerated by the power of myth. At the turn of the century, advertising transformed a largely rural California into a tourist paradise. The entrenchment of the movie industry by the late teens reinforced the region's reputation as a generative source of the American and, by extension, universal urge to pursue a life of leisure.

The urge behind all acts of entertainment is to please the audience, and southern California buildings that are meant as offerings to the idea of a life of relaxation generally exhibit little depth of semantic meaning. Courts are definitely conceived within such intellectual parameters. They express the ideal of entertainment in two important ways: firstly, in the definition of an interior garden space that reflects the possibility of a life outdoors, liberated from the confines of indoor domestic conventions; and, secondly, in the development of the exterior courtyard surfaces of court buildings. The broadly eclectic stylistic nature of such buildings and the thinness and tentative quality of the attachment of their surfaces to the bulk of their mass transfer to these surfaces characteristics of the backdrop or stage set. The dweller is forced to disassociate style as language from building as type and is allowed to engage his or her fantasy by association in the process of giving meaning to buildings whose images transcend their physical reality.

It should be evident by now that we are embarking on this study for reasons that are very explicit. We are concerned with the development of a typological framework of analysis because we value equally style and its inherent symbolic qualities and the construction of the city over time. Both allow the transmission of architectural ideas through the very experience of urban living.

Above left
Arthur B. Zwebell, El Cabrillo, 1928.
The fountain in the courtyard
provided a private oasis and
personal respite from the
uncertainties of the frontier.

Left
Arthur B. Zwebell, El Cabrillo, 1928.
Fragments from the architectural
past gave a civilizing influence to an
evolving city.

Above right
The Hollywood studios of Mary
Pickford and Douglas Fairbanks
showing the sets for the *Thief of
Bagdad*, 1923, a virtual overlap of
real and mythical city. (Courtesy of
The Title Insurance and Trust Co.,
Los Angeles.)

We have chosen to pursue housing because it should be of primary concern to all architects and also because of the current critical housing situation in southern California. We are focusing on indigenous housing prototypes because we believe that they should be preserved. They accurately reflect the historically derived dreams and needs of people of this region; and strengthening them may result in clarifying the urban morphology of the southland in the future. Finally, we have decided to examine courtyard housing critically because it reflects in its form the four principal ideals of southern California culture: the ideal of mobility, the ideal of instant place, the ideal of instant culture, and the ideal of entertainment.

[1] Alan Colquhoun, "Typology and Design Method," *Perspecta* 12 (1969); Aldo Rossi, *L'Architettura della Città* (Padua: Marsilio Editori; S.P.A., 1966).
[2] *Webster's New International Dictionary*, 1960, S.V. *-logy*.

Courtyard Housing as Type

The dominant southern California multifamily dwelling type is the low-rise, high-density courtyard building. There exists a multiplicity of such buildings bound to similarity by the exigencies of the type but displaying a variety of specific solutions brought about by contextual, stylistic, programmatic, and other forces.

The earliest and most numerous examples of courtyard housing are simple repetitions of the single-family house arranged in series. The salient architectural rules of the typology were based on the pragmatics of construction, development, and user expectations. They were actually so obvious and explicit that most courts up to about 1925 were built, not by architects, but by contractors, without reference to standard texts or the consciousness of commonly held values.

As the location, density, and quality of courtyard housing shifted to accommodate an upper-middle-class clientele, however, architects became increasingly involved in their design. It is important to note here that Irving Gill in his Lewis Courts in Sierra Madre (1910) and the Horatio West Courts in Santa Monica (1919), Rudolph Schindler in his proposed Korsen Apartments in Hollywood (1921), and Richard Neutra in the Strathmore Apartments in Westwood (1938) worked within the constraints of a courtyard housing typology.

Despite such occasional brilliant quotes by progressive architects, the overwhelming majority of existing courts are seen in the eyes of visitors, architects, and historians alike as modest buildings unworthy of consideration as architecture. A cursory look at courtyard housing, though, indicates that its formal and spatial qualities depart significantly from typical American dwelling prototypes. It is the space enveloped by the court units that becomes the primary organizing element. In its space rather than object orientation, the courts' sympathies lean toward the traditional city virtues of a defined public realm of streets and squares. The court, then, can be seen as a significant alternative to the illusory American dream of the freestanding house (or apartment house) in the lanscaped park. And any housing prototype that challenges the American intellectual monopoly of the building in the park deserves careful attention and study.

A large proportion of early court dwellers were midwestern retirees on fixed incomes whose quarters were, in most cases, modest one-bedroom or efficiency units. To this day courts function successfully as dwellings for older people. They combine the advantages of compact, easily maintained living quarters with the provision of communal outdoor places for public contact. The emphasis on use of the ground plane minimizes stairs and permits an unusual degree of interaction among people of limited mobility.

The movie industry attracted another large group who made this housing type their home. Hollywood contains colonies of these courts only blocks away from the big studios. One can imagine camera technicians, extras, and maybe even an aspiring Greta Garbo occupying the smaller units. The elaborate versions in West Hollywood became the homes of producers and other movie moguls.

Even today, immigrant and migrant groups have found in the now-old courts a convenient and inexpensive place to live, a way station between a foreign existence (in Asia, Mexico, or New York) and the promised land.

The range of social groups that have occupied and are now living in courts clearly illustrates the universality of the type. The economic or social conditions of the tenants were and are most often reflected in the size and quality of individual units or in the particular tenancy arrangement (ownership versus rental).

The ideal image of the suburban landscape coupled with early building regulations regarding earthquakes kept the courts to a two-story limit. Within these limits courts had no need to advance or radically depart from common building technologies of the period 1910–1930. Western frame and stucco or siding became the standard means of their construction. When a building type is accepted not only as a means of organizing space and form but also as a means of construction, then it enters with particular force into the realm of the builder. The simplicity and inherent economy of the court model caused it to be widely supported by contractors well into the 1930s.

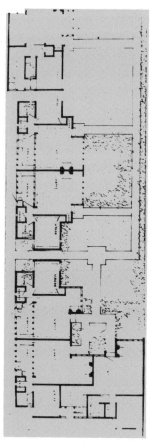

Below
Irving Gill, Horatio West Courts, Santa Monica, 1910, axonometric. (Courtesy of Margaret Bach.)

Below, opposite
Rudolph M. Schindler, plan of projected bungalow court for Jacob Korsen, Los Angeles, 1921. (Courtesy of Schindler Archives, U.C. Santa Barbara.)

Above, opposite
An aerial view of East Hollywood showing a typical concentration of small courts. Notice the group in the center of the picture. Here a group of apartments retains the characteristics of the freestanding house.

Left
The view past the entrance of Casa del Beachwood to the side of the Paramount Studios on Melrose Avenue typifies the proximity of the larger courts and the major motion picture studios.

The California climate has had profound effect upon the architecture of the region, and the courts were no exception. Single-family houses had capitalized on the use of exterior space before the courts, and thus provided a tradition on which the courts could build. Porches, patios, balconies, and various other house extensions all became standard ways to amplify interior spaces. Planting in both semipublic and private spaces became a developed art and contributed to the overall ambience of the court.

High living-room ceilings and cross ventilation became standard ways to offset the effects of dry, hot days and cool nights, the most extreme yearly condition of the southern California climate. The possibility of living indoors or outdoors under pleasant conditions, in natural surroundings, without ever being preoccupied about the weather and its effects, heightened the sense of well-being inherent in court living.

Background

Between 1880 and 1930 the population of the city of Los Angeles doubled every ten years. It reached 1.3 million people at the beginning of the depression.[1] This huge influx of immigrants created an intense demand for housing. The single-family house was most often the typical Los Angeles response towards the accommodation of the newcomers. Even the availability of land and easy mobility, however, could not deter denser clusters in the form of courtyard housing from appearing within the city.

Early land subdivision in southern California favored the single-family dwelling. It was this land parcel, typically 50 by 150 feet, that became the basic unit of development for the courts. Within these land constraints there developed typical court buildings, interspersed with houses and reflecting their basic amenities of privacy and access to open space.

Because of the unobtrusive manner in which courts merged with smaller and less intensively used buildings, they were utilized extensively for spot development without violating the physical and social context of given neighborhoods. Unlike most multifamily dwellings in the United States, the courts expressed in their form little perceivable connotation of class or social status. For that reason they were inhabited by

a great variety of people which changed according to location within the city and the elaboration of accommodations.

Courts are a unique fragment within the city, functioning as an intermediate link between the scale of the individual dwelling and the neighborhood. They recognize two kinds of space: the space they enclose and the outside city space. The severe differentiation between an interior court realm and an exterior city realm allows residential privacy and control and at the same time creates a strong feeling of territoriality.

The courtyard configuration provides opportunities for social interaction; but by drawing the life of courts away from the sidewalk and the street, it can generate a sense of anonymity and disassociation at an urban scale. The integration of the automobile into the court model underlines this aspect. Access to autos within the spatial confines of the building tends to segregate and separate courts from the surrounding city. In a contradictory way that is unique to and characteristic of Los Angeles, the courtyard housing type contains the seeds of both the motel, the ultimate expression of mobility and alienation, and the village green, the traditional American expression of community.

Precedents

The emergence of courtyard housing in Los Angeles is a fact that is supported by a variety of cultural influences and characteristics unique to the region.

The dreaming and pursuit of diverse states of fantasy has been a trademark of southern California since its earliest days. It was this supportive and encouraging attitude toward novelty and cultural hyperbole, as much as the perpetual spring, which brought the movie industry to Los Angeles in the teens. The relationship between the building of movie sets and the building of the city that surrounded the studios is one of mutual dependence.

Most critics believe that insubstantial Los Angeles buildings heavily laden with a variety of styles are a direct derivative of movie-set design and construction. That is not entirely true. Los Angeles finds itself at the western edge of Western culture. For the people who arrived here from the East, adher-

Above left
Arthur B. Zwebell, Patio del Moro, 1925. A typical private patio designed as an extension of the living room.

Above right
Edward Babcock, Casa Torre, Pasadena, 1924. The total landscape of the central courtyard was an important ingredient in defining the quality of the building. Invariably, these landscape schemes were inspired by the hot, dry climate of the region.

Left
Arthur B. Zwebell, Casa Laguna, 1928. The exterior surfaces of the building define the edge of the street. Within is a lush garden.

ence to established symbolic building modes was less important than the generation of a make-believe world that offered instant security and stability.

The financial and material means for instantly producing an observable state of environmental permanence did not exist. The result was the creation of an environment that did not instruct but diverted from the harsh daily realities of a life far away from the seats of power and culture. Diversion happened through delight and deceit. In the absence of any established academic architectural tradition, Los Angeles became an open season for the development of all kinds of theatrical architecture.

There are remarkable examples of how the city actually influenced the design of movie sets. In a region of such stylistic diversity as southern California, a movie director could and still can duplicate in outdoor filming just about any place on earth; but some of the specific examples are quite dramatic. The first Walt Disney studios were situated in Silverlake, on Griffith Park Boulevard. Behind the studios there existed a three-quarter-scale Bavarian village fantasy court constructed in 1928. Could it be on this setting that Disney based his background for his cartoon *Snow White and the Seven Dwarfs* of 1934?[2]

The fact that both set design and most buildings were executed in the same technology—namely, western frame and stucco—accelerated the transference of ideas between sets and architecture. The emergence of historical movie extravaganzas in the late 1920s hastened the pace of the stylistic effect of movies on the city. The growth of extensive libraries in the studios allowed "correct" copying of existing—mostly European, but sometimes exotic—prototypes. When applied to the city, this attitude of correctness limited the possibilities for interpretation of styles and settings and fostered a dry precision in copying that was not unlike the excesses of nineteenth-century European revivalism.

In the exchange and interaction between movie sets and city, a number of generic building types were also transferred into the repertory of the builder, including the Italian country villa with a formal garden; the citified palazzo; the English crescent type, with independent units relating to open spaces assembled into large wholes; and the Spanish urban patio with fountain parterres. These generic ideas were transposed onto new dwelling types, and frequently, by the time they were executed in a specific technology and a specific site, they retained only faint echoes of the original prototypes. The original ideas, nevertheless, dominated the subconscious minds of the builders of the courts.

All the previously mentioned building types are characterized by the definition of a unitary form that encloses an open space and provides for multifamily living. The courts of southern California also allowed their residents to mediate through them their relationship to the larger city structure. If for a moment we imagine the courts as miniaturized English crescents, we can identify in both cases the reading of a whole building in which living units become the constituent cells. At all times, one registers the total building and not merely the sum of its individual parts, thereby compensating for the lack of identity at the smaller scale. Like the middle-class English, the recently arrived Angelenos could indulge their fantasies about the extent of their residences, for it was easy to perceive, in their minds' eyes, all units as parts of the place where they lived.

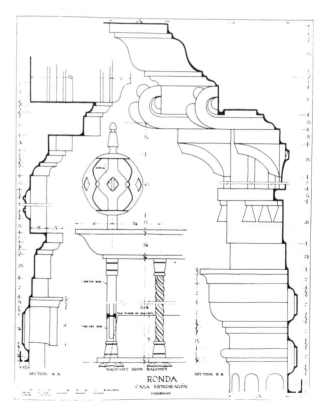

SECTION A.A.   WROUGHT IRON BALCONY   SECTION B.B.

RONDA
CASA MONDRAGÓN
DOORWAY

Above left
The miniature Bavarian Courts built in 1926 on Griffith Park Boulevard just behind the early location of the Disney Studios. Walt Disney may have been a frequent observer of the building during construction. Could this have been the inspiration for some of the scenes in *Snow White and the Seven Dwarfs*?

Above right
The dwarfs' cottage from *Snow White and the Seven Dwarfs*, Walt Disney Studios, 1934–1937.

Below, opposite
Measured drawing of the Mondragon Palace in Ronda, Spain, by Gerstle Mack and Thomas Gibson, 1928. Drawings of this type became the easily accessible models for southern California architects to imitate.

Left
Arthur B. Zwebell, Casa Laguna, 1928. Details of colonnade with upper balcony in the central courtyard copying the typical material mixes (stone and wood) of the region around Granada, Spain.

15

A most important factor that influenced the canonization of courtyard housing as the dominant high-density type in the southland was the proliferation of the wooden bungalow at the turn of the century. The bungalow became one of the most effective and successful means for urbanization in the history of southern California. The reasons are easy to understand. Both as type and as symbol, it fulfilled the needs and dreams of millions as a home with which to begin a new life in California.

Early courts in Echo Park had already capitalized on the individual house as the quantum of courtyard housing typological developments. The form of that house, however, was the sealed box of the East. The coming of the bungalow caused widespread acceptance of the amenities of open space and building extensions into the landscape. The courts designed after 1910 reflect a strong concern with the architectural development not only of the buildings but of the hard and soft landscape, and they begin to introduce the possibility of variation from unit to unit within the confines of a strong overall typological idea. The emergence of the bungalow court marks the beginning of the mature phase of the development of a unique southern California building typology.

Another important local precedent developed because tourism was an important economic underpinning of southern California. Tourism played a dual role as an immediate source of income for Angelenos and as a means of advertising the region and attracting tourists back for a permanent stay. The early building accommodations for tourists included the provision of miniature houses organized around courtyards or loosely arranged in the landscape. These buildings were the seeds of what later became the motel type. It is quite possible that the idea of tents or cabins in the woods organized around a central space was the prototype for this kind of building.

The development and acceptance of the bungalow and its incorporation into tourist courts further expanded the courts' appeal as a means of accommodation unique to the region. The fact that a great many tourists returned to retire in southern California must have encouraged builders to provide permanent high-density accommodations in the original form of the temporary tourist court; and that activity in turn helped to canonize the type and generated a wide range of specific and novel buildings.

The most dominant precedent, from both an organizational and an iconographic point of view, can be described as the Hispanic tradition. California is one of the few states in the United States which was initially colonized by the Spaniards and, subsequently, the Mexicans. Tangible remains of the eighteenth- and nineteenth-century pre-American culture, however, are scarce and hardly suggestive of a glorious past. The network of remaining missions and occasional rancho buildings reflects a limited, isolated, and harsh life, dominated by the reality of agricultural subsistence.

Although the clear development of extraordinary Spanish Revival courts did not occur until the mid-1920s, the operative organizational confines of the Mediterranean urban traditions were evident from the beginning of the courts in the 1880s. Remnants of the mission-rancho heritage persisted in the few original buildings and toponyms that remained. The adobe structures that constituted many of the early buildings of Los Angeles inspired nostalgic attempts to create similar forms and ways of life. More important as a source of nostalgic building images, however, were the missions themselves. Because the missions were accommodations for communities of people living together and isolated in a potentially hostile milieu, a protected form of building naturally emerged. Usually organized around a courtyard space—a cool green space punctuated with a fountain—and usually with arcades or verandas and porches opening directly into this space, the buildings tended to have bland exteriors and active, enriched interiors.

A rural element of genuine Hispanic parentage which also affected the development of the courts was the rancho. As the center of a productive agricultural hinterland, it was made up of a deliberately introverted set of buildings. They defined the spatial nucleus of a small working community of people, and they focused on an open courtyard, an oasis within an uncompromising landscape.

The myth of the need for an indigenous architecture was generated in the late nineteenth century, not by oppressed natives, but by affluent gringos who saw in the idea of "Spanish roots" both an appropriate and a necessary cultural expression. This idea was also used as a legend that became instrumental in the selling of southern California to glamour-starved midwesterners.

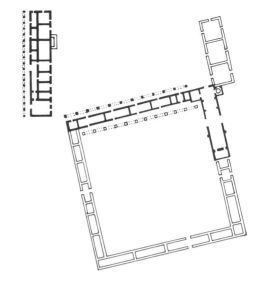

Above left
Heineman Brothers, Bowen Court,
Pasadena, 1912–1913. An example
of a typical bungalow court with
miniature houses defining the central
space.

Left
A typical roadside motel in
Alhambra, California. The form of
early motels is almost identical to
that of courts.

Above right
Mission San Fernando, 1810–22,
plan. Notice the complete enclosure
of the central courtyard.

17

The rediscovery of this mission-rancho background coincided with one of the great real estate booms in American history: between 1883 and 1890, more than 200 towns were platted in Los Angeles County, and the population in southern California increased from 64,000 to 200,000. The mission saga became the operative legend of the southland's urbanization, and the Spanish Revival was established as the preferred building style.[3]

A number of authors have described completely the development of a Mission and subsequently a Spanish Revival architecture.[4] It should suffice to stress here that the alignment with Mediterranean urban landscape and architectural ideas in the period 1890–1930 introduced into southern California cities not only the imagery and common names of the southern Spanish environment but also its typological structure.

In his preface to Austin Whittlesey's book *The Minor Ecclesiastical, Domestic, and Garden Architecture of Southern Spain,* Bertram Goodhue outlines the process by which Andalusia was discovered by young and ambitious American architects.[5] When the traditional grand tour was suspended because of the First World War, Spain became one of the few countries open to architectural touring and study. Traveling architects possessed the theoretical conviction of the desirability of a new southern California architecture based on the eclectic transformation of the forms experienced by the original colonizers of the western United States and Mexico in their native Spain. Such a position had already been formulated by an older generation of California architects. They were also moved by a multitude of romantic accounts of Spain, starting with Washington Irving's *Tales of the Alhambra* of the 1830s and covering the whole range of nineteenth-century Hispanophile literary and musical production. With such substantial motivation, professionals like Whittlesey spent many months in Spain drawing, photographing, and writing about the extraordinary examples of classical and vernacular architecture that they encountered.

Of all the regions of Spain, it was Andalusia that was most visited and most admired, both because of the extreme purity of its settlements and buildings, and because of the climate, landscape, and sharp, clear light that so resembled elements found in southern California.

Above left
Gilmore Adobe, Farmers Market. An adobe dating back to the days of the original Rancho La Brea. The straightforward use of materials and simple architectural forms inspired a good deal of building attempting to capture California's "roots."

Right
Sketch of a doorway in Osuna by Austin Whittlesey from his 1917 tour of Spain. During the First World War, traveling architects shifted their itinerary to the war-free Iberian Peninsula and brought back their discoveries to be admired and duplicated in southern California.

Left
Watercolor by Walter S. Davis of the gate to the Alhambra, Granada. (circa 1911)

DOORWAY - OSVNA
A.W. 1917.

As was customary, long foreign travels led bright, young architects of the teens into substantial practices—except that in this particular case, their practices commenced not only at a time of an exceptional local commercial expansion but also when a new style was needed in order to attach to southern California an identity that could convince the locals and transform the immigrants.

The experience of traveling in southern Spain or the reading about it in published accounts generated two kinds of architecture: architecture born by imitation of the original models, and architecture born by transformation of them. The copying of the original Spanish ideas transplanted into southern California the typological structure of Andalusian cities. And the free interpretation of the physiognomy of southern Spanish buildings generated potent eclectic images that established the so-called Spanish style as the dominant local architectural language. Spanish Revival architecture in southern California can be construed as a series of semantic inventions applied onto the stable body of imported Mediterranean typological models. In a recent trip to Andalusia, we were able to discover and analyze the following courtyard models, from which most southland Spanish Revival court buildings are derived:

1. The urban patio house
2. The *alcazar*
3. The urban palace
4. The urban market and inn
5. The urban *casas de vecinos*
6. The rural *cortijo* or *hacienda*
7. The urban *callejon*

The Urban Patio House

The patio house was the typical instrument of the Greek and Roman colonization of the Iberian peninsula. During the six centuries of Roman domination of the Spanish national space (the second century B.C. to the fifth century A.D.), the patio house also constituted the basic element of urban structure. Finally, during the seven centuries of Arab rule (711 to 1492), the house around a courtyard remained the nucleus of urban building and the measure of urban experience.[6]

In cities with an uninterrupted history of twenty or more centuries, such as Cordoba, one can observe the primacy of the patio house as the most critical shaper of urban form. The elements of the Roman peristyle house are the standard parts of all later sophisticated Andalusian courtyard buildings. The central patio of regular form surrounded by a tile-roofed colonnade, open to the sky, hard paved but enriched by vegetation and water is a distant relative of the West Hollywood deluxe courts. How many unsuspecting Angelenos would ever imagine that the seeds of the places they so love and enjoy living in are intimately connected in their formal derivation to the Roman provincial patio house?

The essence of the court house lies in the definition of an interior landscaped realm separated from the street. This outdoor place is used in the summer as an extension of ground-floor living rooms and is typically furnished with indoor furniture. Occasionally it is covered by a canvas canopy. The court is set apart from the street by an iron gate, which allows the reading of the patio as a partial extension of the city.

The scale of this type of house is generally modest. Its importance does not depend on its monumental qualities but rather arises out of its being repeated as many times as it is necessary in order to define the city. The patio is expressive not only of the primacy of the family as social grouping but also of the intimate nature of its values. The Roman patio is typically regular, the Arab patio often irregular. The difference in shape does not reflect substantial differences in internal typological structure, however; it is an expression of the morphological differences between the Roman gridded city and the Arab irregular and concentric one.

The Alcazar

The urban fortified palaces of the Arab rulers carried the generic name "alcazar." It is imperative to understand that by the year A.D. 1000, at the peak of their glory, the califs of Cordoba were as powerful and sophisticated as the rulers of the Arab kingdoms of their origin in the Middle East. The life of Al-Andalus—the generic Arab name for Andalusia—was based on lucrative agricultural and commercial activities; cultural institutions of the highest order provided an aura of

Right
Roman patio house, Iuliobriga.
Disposed around a central
courtyard, this is the enbodiment of
the urban dwelling in Spain and
much of the Mediterranean.

Below
Patio house in the Barrio de Santa
Cruz, Seville. This is a typical
example of a patio house derived
from Roman sources in one of the old
untouched districts of Seville.

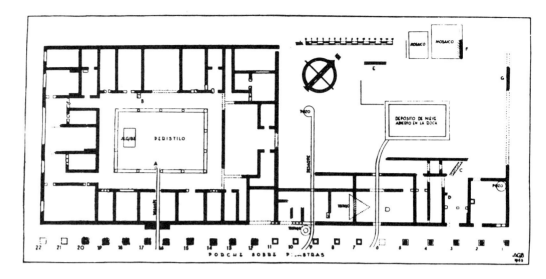

21

liberalism in the midst of absolutist, theocratic values emanating from the alcazars of the rulers.[7]

Perhaps the Arab palace in the Alhambra in Granada is the one that captures most completely the essence of the alcazar as a court prototype. It is made up of a variety of buildings grouped around courtyards. The central courtyard is large but still recognizable as part of an oversized urban patio house. The walls of the palace are blank on the outside, expressing the original defensive nature of the courtyard idea. The landscape of the interior courtyards is carried out in an extraordinary manner, with sky, water, and silence as the three most powerful compositional (im)materials. Many kinds of rooms open directly into the courtyards, and various second-story rooms connect visually through windows and balconies. The patio-defining walls are delicate in color and detail, suggesting a very soft outer boundary to the space of the courtyard.

The alcazars were occupied by the rulers and their families (harems) and can therefore be considered as a multifamily housing type. The dimensions and proportions of the exterior spaces and the purity of landscape render the alcazar a powerful transformational prototype, one that is clearly linked to the mature courts of southern California.

The Urban Palace

In the process of the reconquest of Andalusia from the thirteenth century to the fifteenth century, the land of the vanquished Moors was handed over to the victorious Christian soldiers. The noble leaders of the Christian armies won enormous political power and influence. They established themselves in the newly liberated lands and erected for themselves urban palaces of great opulence but of lesser scale than the Arab alcazars.[8]

The typological structure and scale of these palaces closely resemble those of the elaborate courts of southern California. Whereas the urban court house and the alcazar were transformed into the unique California court building type, urban palaces, such as the Casa de los Tiros in Granada and the Palacio Mondragon in Ronda, were actually transferred into their American context in their entirety.

A number of important issues highlight the pragmatics of this transference. The palaces make public urban space, such as the street, courtyards, and back-lot gardens, while at the same time their own mass is strongly defined in space. The building details, both constructed and applied, picturesquely reflect the process of assembling and maintaining the palaces over a long period of time. The eclectic superposition of architectural fragments often brings classical and Moorish details into direct contact. Typical elements can be observed in the courtyards—wells, benches, platforms, planters, fountains, balustrades, gates, and the like. The landscape, both soft and hard, natural and artificial, is developed into a significant design protagonist. The life in these palaces was complex, just as the places provided inside them were diverse. The scale of both the buildings and the experience within them was larger than that of the extended-family house. The palaces, therefore, became microcosms of the city. Over the centuries, many of these grand houses of the aristocracy were subdivided and were—and still are—occupied by many families. It is not atypical for one palace to house between fifteen and twenty families today.

All the above factors facilitated the importation of the palace model into southern California as an appropriate multifamily housing instrument and caused it to become popular and successful.

Below, opposite
The Generalife, Granada, circa 1240, plan.

Below left
Court of the Myrtles, the Alhambra, Granada, 1334–1354. This is the classic example of the urban Arab palace courtyard.

Below right
Casa de los Tiros, Granada, 1505. This typical urban palace is a royal-scaled building compared to the patio house.

Right
Measured drawings of the courtyard of the Casa Mondragon, Ronda, by Gerstle Mack and Thomas Gibson, 1928.

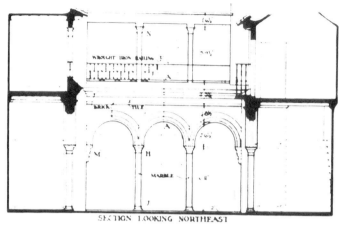

SECTION LOOKING NORTHEAST

The Market and the Inn

A number of public or commercial activities have been accommodated by courtyard buildings since the Arab days in Andalusia. The *zoco* is the traditional Arab market, a fine example of which survives in Cordoba. It is made up of three courtyards of differing dimensions and qualities, and most probably it was occupied by workshops and commercial establishments. What is important about the zoco model is, firstly, its multicourtyard definition and, secondly, the fact that the courtyards are always expressed as regular voids (typically squares in plan) in sites that are most often irregular. Place is established as a measure of both dimension and regularity of shape.

The Arab urban inns, of which two wonderful examples remain—the Posada del Potro in Cordoba and the Casa del Carbon in Granada—are spatially organized in ways similar to those in which high-density dwellings are organized. The arrangement of repetitive living units around a courtyard—as in the motels of today—and the scale of mass and void of these inns provided clear clues for possible imitation. Landscape is not treated prominently, but the urban dimensions of these buildings are crucial as precedents to Los Angeles courts. The existence of articulated entranceways or the differentiation between the ground floors—reserved for animals—and the upper stories—to be used for living—suggest strong connections with Los Angeles multiuse courts.

The Casas de Vecinos

As a housing model, the casas de vecinos correspond closely to a pure Andalusian equivalent to southern California courts. The casas de vecinos are apartment houses developed around the principle of a shared courtyard from the mid–eighteenth century on. When they incorporate as a formal element a second-story circulation gallery, they are called *corrales*.[9]

The urban dimensions of the casas de vecinos resemble in general terms those of the palaces. Unique typological features emerge at the scale of building and landscape. The buildings are subdivided into dwellings that are not expressed as separate units in space. Their mass rarely exceeds two stories, and the dwellings are as much as

possible related to the ground. Strongly positive central spaces are made by the buildings that surround them; in general the semantic dimension of the courtyards of casas de vecinos arises out of the enumeration of and relationships among the basic architectural elements that bound them. Doors, windows, staircases, walls, balconies, and arcades are used as the means to express the appropriate degree of publicness or privacy of the various parts of the courtyards.

As far as the landscape of these buildings is concerned, specific elements of communal living, such as wells, *lavaderos,* mailbox clusters, niches with the holy figurines, benches, fountains, and planters, serve as the standard parts of a typological repertory. Not only are these elements thoroughly repeated in Andalusian casas de vecinos into the twentieth century, but also they were imported into southern California as the necessary elements of the mature Spanish Colonial Revival courts.

The casas de vecinos can be found in both large and small southern Spanish cities. Depending on their particular site, they are carried out either in a formal style—obviously designed by an architect—or in the simple vernacular forms of the region. It is important to know that both from an organizational and stylistic point of view, vernacular courtyard housing was recognized by Modern architects in Spain.[10] The typological lessons of the courts were lost, however, in the torrent of modern propaganda emanating principally from Paris and Berlin.

The Cortijo or Hacienda

The two words *cortijo* and *hacienda* refer to the same building idea: the isolated and freestanding farm complex in whose confines both production and living take place. The word *hacienda* is used when the farm is connected with the cultivation of olives. The word *cortijo* refers to all other types of farms.[11]

The scale of the cortijo as a built object is considerably larger than that of the prototypes already examined. In the barren and rolling agricultural landscape of Andalusia, its precise square-walled configuration sets it up almost as a fortress. Its white color contrasts sharply with the colors of the land and the sky.

Below right
The Zoco, or Arab market, in Cordoba. The stable, regular space of the interior courtyard belies the confusion of the Arab casbah beyond.

Below left
Casa del Carbon, Granada, early fourteenth century. A famous example of an Arab inn.

Right
Casa de vecinos, Granada. Developed in the eighteenth century, these dwellings are literally apartment houses that surround a commonly shared space.

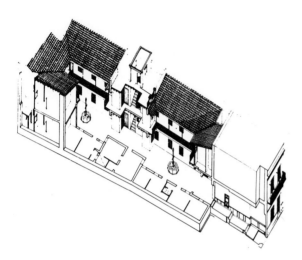

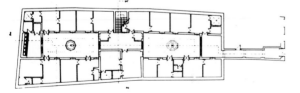

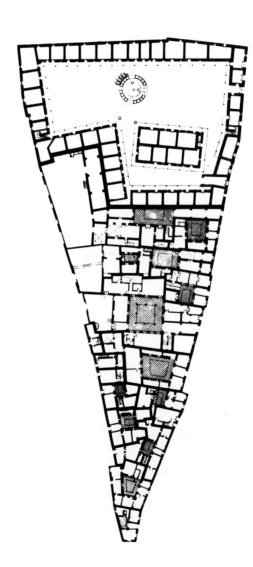

Top
Plan of the Hacienda Micones in the province of Seville. Note the increasing density of walls as one moves outward from the center. (From Carlos Flores, *Arquitectura Popular Española*, p. 224.)

Bottom
Cortijo near Ronda. The isolated building grouping invariably surrounds a protected interior space where farm production and living activities take place.

Two important facts make the cortijos important precedents to the Los Angeles courts. Firstly, because many of them were designed by architects and built over long periods of time as agricultural needs changed, they possess extraordinarily picturesque massing and evocative details. These volumetrically pure building complexes moved the sensibilities of southern California architects during their Andalusia trips.

Secondly, the cortijos were to be found in the countryside, isolated from the change-inducing influences of the city. Both the life and the forms of the cortijos conserve the simplicity of rural existence and the purity of vernacular form. Their effect as objects suggestive of a romantic fugue must have been supreme. They still surprise the visitor with the boldness of their forms and their dominance over the landscape.

A number of other specific Spanish Revival transferences can be traced back to the cortijo. The highly articulated entranceway, the watchtower, and the shaded courtyard are all integral parts of the Andalusian prototype. The entranceway, that most exaggerated Spanish preoccupation, here clearly differentiates the occupied interior realm from the wild outdoors. The tower is a leftover element from the days of insecure countryside living which stretch back from the nineteenth century to the first recorded beginnings of life around the Mediterranean. The trees in the courtyard are related to the necessity for shade. Andalusia is hot and dry in the summer, and life is hardly possible without respite from the sun.

The cortijo as court precedent is doubly important, for it influenced the design of courtyard housing directly and also indirectly. It is clearly the dominant building precedent for the design of southern California missions and ranchos, both of which are in their own right formal antecedents of courtyard housing.

The Urban Callejon

The callejon is a dead-end urban street, typical of the Arab cities of southern Spain. Although made up of different buildings, the street of that scale surrounded by doors and windows of many attached houses became the actual and

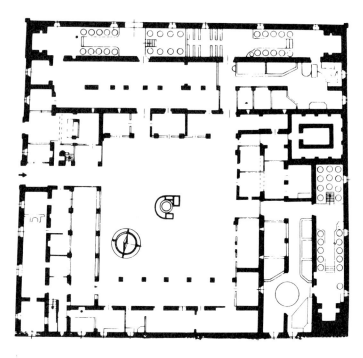

Top
Plan of the Hacienda Micones in the province of Seville. Note the increasing density of walls as one moves outward from the center. (From Carlos Flores, *Arquitectura Popular Española*, p. 224.)

Bottom
Cortijo near Ronda. The isolated building grouping invariably surrounds a protected interior space where farm production and living activities take place.

symbolic embodiment of the possibility of public action and representation.[12]

Not unlike the primitive first courts of Los Angeles, the initial formulation of the courtyard as place is none other than the street. Although in many parts of Spain streets can be interpreted as courtyards, one contemporary example in Cordoba is outstanding in its suggestiveness as an example of this model. The Casa del Indiano was a mere facade when it was salvaged in the early 1970s by having an actual court as street built behild it. The regularity of entrances, the repetitiveness of architectural elements, and the quality of the streetscape combine to provide a fine illustration of the organizational and expressive possibilities of the thin, narrow courtyard as place.

Of all the models examined above, the urban callejon provided the least inspiration to the architects of the Spanish Revival. As a type of urban building, however, it is so simple and powerful that it served as the basis for the urbanization of large tracts of land through popular housing in South and Central America and, by extension, in southern California. The callejon constitutes the most direct ancestor to the majority of the Los Angeles courts of the working class at the turn of the century.

There is one factor that remains underexposed in the context of such overwhelming evidence of cultural connections between southern California and southern Spain, and that is the possible links of precedents between our region and Mexico or Central America. It is a fact that in the 1920s a number of source books were written about vernacular Mexican architecture and the possibilities of its application in southern California.[13] Clearly the most important tie, though, was that many of the mature deluxe courts were actually constructed by imported Mexican or Chicano artisans and laborers, at home with the imagery and in part the technology of the Spanish Revival. And a large portion of the materials used for the construction and embellishment of these courts— primarily tiles—were fabricated south of the border and transported to Los Angeles.

In conclusion, the conscious and unconscious factors that generated the courts are so thoroughly interrelated that it is difficult to qualify them and judge their relative importance with precision. It is undoubtedly true that they gave rise to a multiple-family dwelling type that was uniquely suited to the ways of life and the stylistic expectations of millions of new Californians. The precedents outlined above, whether imitated or transformed, were so originally and cleverly manipulated that the architectural quality of many courts is still apparent today. Whether as spatial organizational idea, landscape, decipherable form, or city fragment, courtyard housing is still an active, valuable ingredient in the Los Angeles environment.

[1] Carey McWilliams, *Southern California: An Island on the Land* (Salt Lake City: Peregrine-Smith, 1973), p. 113.

[2] Christopher Finch, *The Art of Walt Disney* (Burbank: Walt Disney Productions, 1975), pp. 65–76.

[3] McWilliams, pp. 118–125.

[4] David Gebhart, "The Spanish Colonial Revival in Southern California (1895–1930)," *Journal of the Society of Architectural Historians,* May 1967, pp. 131–47; Harold Kirker, *California's Architectural Frontier* (San Marino, Calif.: Huntington Library, 1970), pp. 120–130; McWilliams, pp. 70–83.

[5] Bertram Goodhue, preface to *The Minor Ecclesiastical, Domestic, and Garden Architecture of Southern Spain,* by Austin Whittlesey (New York: Architectural Book Publishing, 1923), pp. V–VIII.

[6] Marquesa de Casa Valdes, *Jardines de España* (Madrid: Aquilar Ediciones, 1976), pp. 3–17.

[7] G. A. Garcia de Cortaza, *La España Medieval,* Historia de España Alfaguarra, vol. 2 (Madrid: Alianza Editorial, 1976), chaps. 1 and 2.

[8] Francisco Collantes de Teran Delorme and Luis Gomez Estern, *Arquitectura Civil Sevillana* (Seville: Ayuntamiento de Sevilla, 1976).

[9] Luis Feduchi, *Arquitectura Popular Española* (Barcelona: Los Pueblos Blancos, Editorial Blume, 1978), 4:257.

[10] *AC/GATEPAC 1931–37* (Barcelona: Editorial Gili, 1975), no. 18, pp. 14–37.

[11] Feduchi, pp. 251–254.

[12] Antonio Garcia y Bellido et al., *Resumen Historico del Urbanismo en España* (Madrid: Instituto de Estudios de Administracion Local, 1968), pp. 73–74, 88–94.

[13] Richard Garrison and George Rustay, *Mexican Houses* (New York: Architectural Book Publishing, 1930).

Below
A callejon in Cordoba, behind the
facade of the Casa del Indiano.
These streets become a kind of
extended urban courtyard.

Below
Cordoba, plan of the city near the
Mezquita, 1811, showing the typical
Arab dead-end streets, or
callejones. (From Antonio Garcia y
Bellido et al., *Resumen Historico de
Urbanismo en España*, p. 82.)

3

In order to recognize a building as part of a courtyard-housing typology, one has to define the typology's constituent rules. The definition depends on the description of building and space elements and the assignment of relationships between them.

First, there is a central courtyard, a regularly configured public open space, which provides both access and a realm for public activity. Its plan shape is typically rectangular and its ground is carefully divided into hard and soft landscaping in order to direct movement, to screen dwellings, or merely to embellish. The means of access are rigidly defined in spatial terms. Pedestrian access is incorporated into the courtyard, and vehicular access is usually outside and peripheral. This basic differentiation defines in the dwellings a front and a back, a public and a service side. The internal structure of the dwellings is dominated by these rules of access. The width of the courtyard, its relationship to the dwellings, and its connection to the city beyond determine whether it is used as a contemplative place or merely as a route for pedestrian circulation. The surfaces (elevations and landscape) surrounding the courtyard, if treated as a continuous fabric, act as an evocative backdrop to the life of the court. They are the most elaborately styled surfaces of the buildings, in contrast to plain fronts and even more plain side service yards or backyards.

Second, dwellings are arranged around the court. Whether attached or detached, single story or maisonette, they are dominated by the ground plane and the living amenities inherent in it. There is direct access from all dwellings, whether ground or upper level, to the ground. The passage from court to building or from level to level is always articulated as portico, porch, front yard, or stair. Within the limited space of the court, building elements express or generate specific realms of activity or experience. Individual units vary considerably from court to court. Many of them have extremely small efficiency units consisting of living/dining room, kitchen, bedroom, and bathroom. Larger courts have elaborate accommodations of up to three or four bedrooms and demonstrate variations in planning according to view, orientation, topography, and similar factors. Despite these var-

Above left
A typical court in Hollywood, circa 1920.

Above right
A downhill court in Echo Park is formed by the stepped aggregation of simple house units.

Left
Site plan from Walter S. Davis et al., *Ideal Homes in Garden Communities* (Los Angeles: Garden City Company of California, 1915).

iations, the living spaces are always oriented toward the major central space, while services, such as kitchen or bathroom, line the sides and rear.

Size differences aside, all units, whether attached or detached, consciously attempt to duplicate the amenities of the detached single-family house. Equivalence of dwelling standards is characteristic of most courts.

Third, courts integrate the car without allowing it to tyrannize the dwelling. Parking garages often occur in the rear with side service driveway; direct-access garages occur directly off the street on sloping sites; larger courts have group garages hollowed out under the central courtyard. In these ways, the automobile is incorporated into the complex without intruding upon open space. It is important to recognize that the accommodation of the car in this building type occurred as early as the mid-1920s. This accommodation is quite a radical departure in the history of residential building, and it reflects the unique admiration, acceptance, and love of automobiles that has characterized this region's culture for over sixty years.

The definition of a public and a service zone for each dwelling is articulated through the provision of threshold elements on both front and back. These elements are either spatial extensions of the dwelling or building elements such as overhangs, stairs, or stoops. The gradation of experience from the outside to the inside in each dwelling is important in increasing the viability of dwellings as independent living units in a medium-to-high-density situation. Also, the repetition of such elements as pedimented overhangs over entries, porches, window grills, and elaborate downspouts provides important orientational clues that direct the visitor and resident toward appropriate movement or intended significance.

The typical courtyard housing scheme is distorted by dimensional variation of all the zones, both vertical and horizontal. This variation generally depends on numerous factors, including site size, access to light and sun, access to street, view, and topography. The vertical zone has been found in one-story, two-story, and three-story configurations, while the horizontal zone has been observed to exist in the following dimensional ranges: courtyard, 8–75 feet; threshold, 0–6 feet; dwelling, 12–35 feet; service, 0–4 feet; and garage, 8–10 feet.

The combination of zones of varying dimensions produces a rich variety of specific courtyard housing examples. The range of possible partis or overall spatial configurations is affected by three factors: access; the relationship of courtyard to street and parked car; and the ratio of building to open space. The diagrams that follow describe the range of basic partis that we have observed in southern California. Each variance retains the basic zoning of the courtyard housing idea and reflects the discipline of the overall typology.

The Single-Bar Parti

The single bar is the oldest and most elementary parti we discovered. Technically it does not even define a courtyard except that in a city situation, the space between the building and its neighbors assumes the quality of a formed outdoor place. It is a pretty rare type to observe because most often buildings of this kind are added to and are transformed over time into higher-order partis.

Detached-unit courts of this type represent the most primitive attempts to create high-density housing in southern California. The detached units are patterned after individual houses. They are invariably very small and most often identical to one another; few architectural articulations are used to create defined outdoor private spaces. The building technology typically utilized is wood frame and wooden siding or shingles, which leads us to believe that this courtyard housing variety is indeed the oldest in the region. Cars are not properly accommodated in the single-bar type, possibly because most bars of this kind were constructed before the introduction and widespread use of the automobile.

Attached-unit courts of this type offer a richer set of examples than detached units, primarily because they have been considered and executed as single buildings capable of integrating sophisticated architectural ideas. The most interesting examples observed were attached single-bar buildings that were sited on sloping terrain, thus offering the possibility of sectional variation and contextual response. Sectional variation allows a vertical shifting of the court in parts so that light and views can become available to the units located along the slope. Often the terracing of land makes feasible the provision of private yards (living or service) for each unit in the court. Even the car is accommo-

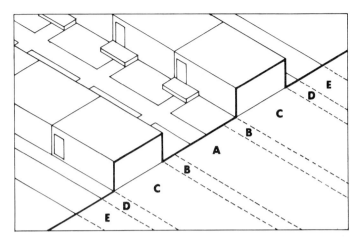

Above left
A small court at 534–538 Kingsley Drive, Hollywood, showing a typical scenic drive leading to parking garages in the rear.

Left
A Hollywood court; typical threshold elements (porches, stairs, hedges) mediate the space between the dwelling and the courtyard.

Above right
Basic zoning idea. *A*, court; *B*, threshold; *C*, unit; *D*, service; *E*, vehicular access.

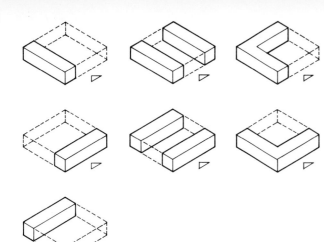

Opposite
In a typical Hollywood street of small houses, each house is detached from the street by a landscaped zone. Cars are limited to the street and are parked in the rear of the houses. The sidewalk is articulated as a distinct public pedestrian zone.

A   B   C   D   E

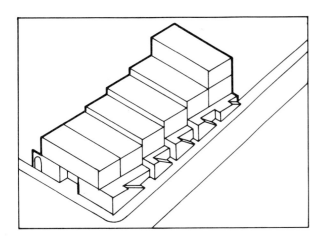

Top
Courtyard housing, organizational typology. A single-bar type; B, L type; C, double-bar type; D, U type; E, completed courtyard type.

Above right
Typical single-bar court in Echo Park.

Above left
Single-bar court, 1327–1339 Lilac Terrace, Echo Park, diagram.

dated (at street level) within rare single-bar attached courts on sloping sites.

Often these buildings are placed on corner sites so that the street assumes the role of the courtyard. Interesting porch, stair, and stoop additions on their public side make their overall form complex and animate the life of the street. In situations where land use changes at street level, these courts can accommodate special, nondwelling types of structures, such as small workshops or shops. Finally, because these latter single-bar parti examples have been thought of as a building and because they are carried out in a wood-frame technology, their exterior surfaces begin to reflect particular stylistic predilections. The examples found in the parts of Los Angeles urbanized at the turn of the century are most often carried out in a Shingle style or Mission Revival idiom.

The Double-Bar Parti

The double-bar parti is a rare one, especially because in terms of the transformational sequences of the courtyard housing typology it is an intermediate stage leading to the most common court, the U-configuration building. Its value lies in that, especially in the case of the detached-unit model, it directly reflects the immediate formal derivation of the courtyard housing type from the typical suburban street. In the literal translation of a street into a courtyard through the shrinkage of the scale of houses and the spaces that surround them, one loses the plushness of accommodation but retains the reading of the house as the ultimate dwelling symbol and of the neighborhood as the most desirable entity expressive of collective values.

The double-bar parti within a typical Los Angeles middle-of-the-block lot appears pretty commonly. The courtyard is exceptionally narrow, too narrow to permit a developed sense of landscape or rich private extensions off the individual units. The units remain repetitive efficiency or one- or two-bedroom packages of exceptionally tight space standards, unable to adjust architecturally to the automobile. With few exceptions, these courts are still in the realm of cheap housing, to the point of sacrificing basic living amenities.

The only important buildings of this kind occur where distortions are induced into the type because of topography or

Above and left
In the transformation of the street into a double-bar court, first the street is reduced into a passage, and its ground surface is abridged with only two tracks remaining for overlapped pedestrian and vehicular use. Then the car is removed entirely from the space between dwellings, and a formed, landscaped courtyard emerges.

context. In the case of detached-unit courts, a corner site can allow the addition of multiple side entrances and access into the central courtyard space. In rare cases of mid-block location, especially in Hollywood, courts placed across from each other along a street begin to suggest complex pedestrian passages. They bypass the stiff structure of the city block and introduce the possibility of labyrinthine movement in the city.

Sloping sites permit sensitive articulations of the domain of the individual dwellings. The unavailability of an alley for access and parking can transform the central courtyard into a hard motor court, a convenient reminder that the double-bar parti is directly related formally to the cul-de-sac street.

Countless variations of the double-bar parti theme allow for minimalist economy versions (below left), apartments on sloping sites (left), especially in Echo Park, and even five-story-high brick courts, like the Villa Elena in Hollywood (below right).

The L Parti

The L parti is the first in the series we are examining which begins to define the enclosure of the courtyard by means of the building form. A few archaic examples of this type exist in the Echo Park district of Los Angeles, where the units remain detached. Especially when located on a sloping site, such courts suffer from a weak overall definition of the central courtyard.

The later attached-unit examples, however, show clearly the role of discreet architectural elements in the development of dominant outdoor spaces. A courtyard conceived as a positive public element introduces into buildings a sense of order and ceremony which causes an immediate differentiation between their formal and informal, front and back, public and service aspects. The net effects of such a differentiation are that cars are banished behind the legs of the L or underneath the courtyard and that the surfaces of the buildings surrounding the courtyards begin to assume a stylistic presence that reflects concerns not limited to the expression of the exigencies of the single dwelling. Units in such buildings are invariably complex, not necessarily repetitive, and often disguised in their outward appearance. Entrances, stairs, front yards, doors, windows, roofs, and similar elements are strongly articulated.

Typically, L courts open up to the street, most probably in order to conceal automobiles behind the bar of the leg farthest from the street. In doing so, such buildings become substantial offerings to the city, as their large, open, and pleasantly landscaped courtyards open directly to the sidewalk and substantially expand the public realm.

One of the peculiar contradictions inherent in this kind of court is the common occurrence of two courtyards symmetrically related but with no stated or obvious connection to each other. Occasionally neighboring courtyards happen to be surrounded by buildings whose exterior surfaces express disparate stylistic and organizational concerns. In such cases it becomes clear that the L parti is far from being a complete, self-sufficient model and can be considered as a type in transformation, again leading to a parti of a higher order.

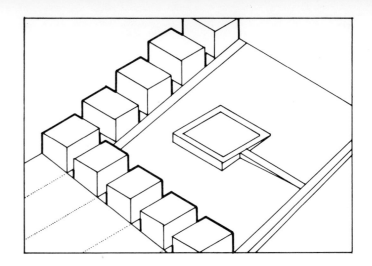

Above
The L-type court, diagram.

The U Parti

The U parti is the most common and typical idea for a courtyard housing scheme. Because of the great number of observed examples of this kind (fully 80 percent of all known courts in Los Angeles are of the U-parti kind), there appear interesting variations of the original idea.

The most telling aspect of this type is its transformation from a detached-unit, single-story building to an attached-unit, two-story, completed courtyard building. This transformation is instrumental in describing the development of the type from its primitive beginnings to its sophisticated and most mature manifestations.

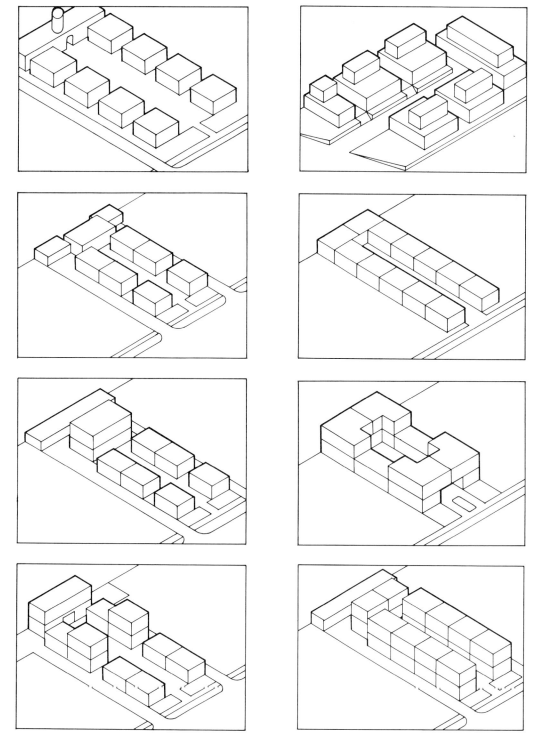

Right
The transformation of the U-parti type courts from a detached-unit, single-story building to an attached, two-story building. (Based on observed Los Angeles court examples.)

39

Below left
Courtyard view of a typical
single-story U court.

Below right
Courtyard view of a typical two-story
U court.

Left
Side view of a court with an irregular
massing profile.

Left
Variations of the downhill U-parti
court type as observed in the Echo
Park district of Los Angeles.

41

Another source of formal diversity is topography. Because much of the growth of Los Angeles occurred near the hills surrounding downtown, courts had to adjust themselves to topographical constraints. The most typical uphill or downhill buildings provide for the parking of cars in enclosed garages on street level and then generate terraces, shared by at least two units, out of the hillsides. This breaking up of the courtyard into many parts at different levels, usually connected but discontinuous, results in a strong articulation of the immediate relationship between the dwelling and the courtyard.

Other interesting side effects of the U downhill courts include the spectacular views they offer into the valleys surrounding them and the fine light they may receive (depending on their orientation), since their overall form permits penetration of the sun's rays.

Most U-parti examples, especially the ones constructed at the turn of the century as cheap housing for new immigrants, follow the unit type patterns of the previously discussed partis. The units are uniform, repetitive, and spatially very tight indeed. Later, though, especially in the late 1920s, there arose another type of court on the U parti which departed fundamentally from earlier examples. What characterized these second- and third-generation courts is variation in section, both at the level of the whole building and at the level of the dwellings themselves. The result is the development of new courtyard housing prototypes that offer a complex, occasionally picturesque massing with a variety and diversity of dwelling units, and even of uses, within them. In rare and very well developed cases, no two units within a court are the same.

Courts of this kind are surrounded on three sides by buildings and most typically are located with their open end facing the street. Often the front of the court at the street is completed with a thin wall screen connecting the two front bars of the U. The definition of the courtyard is powerful, and, if the width and the shape of the site allow, the courtyard can be given qualities and character as a substantial landscape element. There are three kinds of courtyards in this type: the ones that serve merely as passage; the ones that are more generous, but simply define the courtyard as the sum of the pieces belonging to individual units; and the ones that offer a developed and independently formed courtyard with no

Below left
Terraced U-parti courts on Echo Park Lake.

Below right
U-type court on a sloping site with garages.

Right
Multiuse terraced courts on Sunset Boulevard in Echo Park.

focus on any one unit. Within all three types, individual entrances into units are typically articulated, as are other important building elements. It is actually highly instructive that the celebration of the uniqueness of these building elements (stairs, doors, windows, and so on) comes about only when a stable and observable parti is established.

The dominant technology in the construction of these courts is wood frame; therefore, with the numbers of examples of this kind of parti available, the stylistic range we have observed is extraordinary. It would be fair to say that following on the example of single-family houses at this time, every single historical style is represented—both occidental and oriental, both vernacular and erudite, both ancient and modern. One is faced here, not with academic issues of revivalism of styles, but with full-fledged style wars.

One of the factors that causes special distortions in the U-parti courts is the car. It has been mentioned before that in cases of uphill courts, the car is often nestled underneath the first terrace. There exist many other ingenious ways of accommodating the car within this type. Vehicular access typically occurs on the edges of sites. Therefore, cars are often parked in separate structures on the sides or on the backs of buildings, or in uncommon but interesting cases they are accommodated within particular parts (especially in the back) of the bars that form the U building. In rare and exceptional cases the car is placed underneath the courtyard. It is, of course, obvious that in many turn-of-the-century courts and those built before 1920, the car is not accommodated at all.

Increased density requirements forced the intensification of building within the court envelope. The massing transformation of courts within the U confines has already been discussed. Another kind of transformation that is equally interesting is the one that begins to distort the U parti into a higher-order type, typically the closed courtyard type. A number of observed examples illustrate this point. Especially in situations of generous courtyards, the bars of the U begin to turn the corner as if to suggest the ultimate act of enclosure.

Top
The street is often defined by the connection of the two wings of the typical U court with a screen wall.

Above and right
The courtyard in its simplest form is a passage. It is later transformed into a space dependent on the dwelling unit and finally becomes a stable, fully formed exterior public room.

The Completed Courtyard Parti

The completed courtyard parti is the most accomplished realization of the court typology. The public exterior space is given total definition as an enclosed landscaped place, with the city in all its manifestations definitely excluded.

The parti is strong enough to accept access from two sides, most often two adjacent ones, and still retain the integrity of the central space. Typically, the central space is a regular grid, a rectangle or square dimensioned in such a way as to accept a fountain in its center as a major object of sizable volume. Surrounding surfaces are most often two stories in height and incorporate architectural elements at diverse scales. For instance, communal fireplaces reflecting the scale of the whole courtyard and major entrance doorways reflecting the scale of a whole unit are common. The courtyard always insistently expresses the imagery of the communal living room.

Most of these buildings are located on flat sites. Rarely are major completed courtyard parti buildings distorted by topography. When that occurs, the difference in level is taken up as an architectural element in the courtyard and is hidden in the body of the building itself. The closed court located on the flat precludes major views from the buildings to their surroundings and implies inward, introspective qualities.

The massing of such buildings tends to be complex, both as a reflection of picturesque intentions in the composition of exteriors and also because of the tremendous diversity in the organization of living units. Double-story living rooms, exterior porches, yards, and balconies are common, but, most importantly, rarely are two units similar. Space standards are ample; densities are quite high, reaching up to thirty dwellings per acre; and on a given site housing is always the only use.

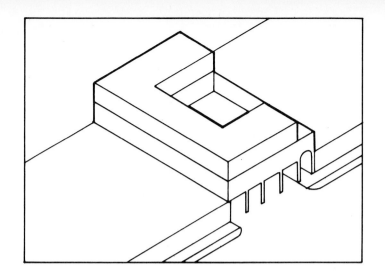

Above
An example of the transformation of the U-parti court type toward a fully enclosed courtyard type.

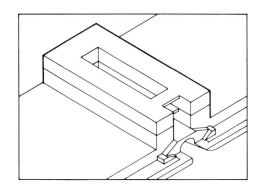
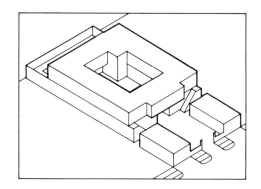

Left
Variations of the denser and more
elaborate completed courtyard type
found primarily in West Hollywood.

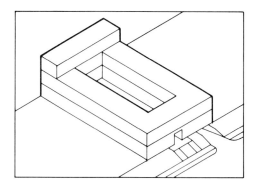
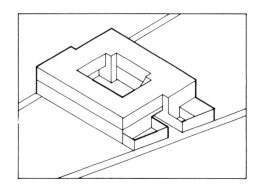

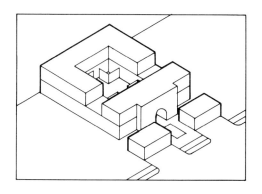
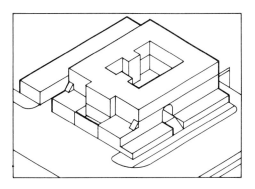

The car, which is diversely accommodated, generates some of the most basic distortions of the completed-courtyard parti. Most commonly, parking is located underneath the buildings. Such an innovation for buildings constructed as early as 1925 was a major contribution to the world body of developing housing ideas. In a substantial number of other cases, the car is accommodated outside the domain of the central courtyard by major additions to the main building. Garages are used as means to create an independent car domain, to complete the space available in irregular sites, or to take advantage of alleys or special access opportunities in corner sites.

The imagery of these highly elaborated courtyard housing examples is decidedly Spanish Revival, but as the names of most buildings reveal, their source is rather decidedly urban Mediterranean vernacular. The unique aspect of this revivalism lies in the fact that the authors of the deluxe courts aimed to express in their buildings something beyond mere eagerness to reproduce details of southern European building prototypes. They actually attempted to create substantial urban fragments that would suggest in that climate and at that nostalgia-saturated time the possibility of being in the Mediterranean. It is for this reason that the interior elevations of many courts appear to be discontinuous and made up of clashing, disparate parts simulating the growth of an urban whole over time. The compulsive concern with urban fragments as opposed to single buildings led architects to a precise definition of the public urban elements (such as street plants, ground finishes, balustrades, and roofs) on whose definition the positive reading of overall environmental quality often rests and on which the eliciting of fantasy-related responses to places also depends.

Where courts of this kind are found close to each other in the city, they suggest an inward, closed world separated from the street. One begins to get a reading of a neutral exterior urban space, left empty for the benefit of vehicles and representing some kind of stiff, formal public behavior, while behind the walls of the courts lurk all the forbidden temptations to act privately and freely.

Above
The courtyard of Arthur B. Zwebell's
the Andalusia, 1927.

Multiple/Special Partis

In a small number of buildings, the completed-courtyard parti is multiplied or distorted by unique contextual conditions. Such cases, few as they are, offer the best illustration of the capability of a Los Angeles building to equal the urban structure and living amenities of Andalusian towns.

Where two spaces exist as separate domains (Ronda), they are expressed as two diametrically opposed architectural entities. The hard-soft, city-country, leisure-working courtyard idea is carried out in a way that generates substantial variety of places and multiplies the possibilities of diverse experiences within the buildings.

When a great many spaces are organized without a defined center but all flowing into each other (Cadiz), the idea of a courtyard building as village finds its purest realization. The continuity of surfaces surrounding the courtyard, the turning of corners without evidence of their being terminated, suggests a street scene. The hard landscape of the courtyard further heightens the sense of exterior public Mediterranean urban space. The seeming irregularity of projecting building volumes and elements perhaps aims to simulate the structure of a medieval city, spontaneously generated and developed with discipline of form and construction.

In the case of a variety of small public courtyards organized around a main movement path (Roman Gardens), one gets the strongest possible hint of labyrinthine space. It is not a Casbah that is suggested here, but a Venetian cityscape with extraordinary campos of many sizes and qualities opening up to the right and left of the observer in every path in the city. The possibility of relating units to minicourts within a single building heightens the sense of identity of the inhabitants and generates a diversity of accommodation which is amazing if one considers the limits of land and building mass available.

Occasionally courtyards are placed in series next to each other. When that schema is coupled with a use mix (residential and commercial) and an unusual height definition (four stories), the ingredients of an extraordinary building are set into motion (Granada). The courtyard and the surfaces that enclose it constitute a precise attempt to recreate a street scene with all its variety of formal definition and accommodation of disparate activity. Where the interior courtyard

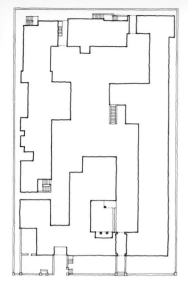

expresses the structure of the single commercial establishment, the exterior of the building on the actual street side reflects the scale of a southern Spanish urban fragment. There is no evidence of the spatial structure of the building in the massing or detail; and every architectural hint points in the direction of breaking down the scale of the building blocks into smaller imaginary architectural components.

In the rare case where a completed-courtyard parti is placed in an irregular and at the same time sloping site, it generates a building of multiple dimensions that again simulates accurately an urban scene (Villa Madrid). The central courtyard is

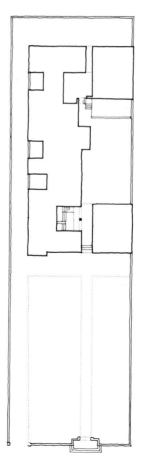

Above left
Milton Black, El Cadiz, 1936, organizational diagram.

Below left
Milton Black, El Cadiz, 1936. The central courtyard in terms of its proportions and finishes is transformed into a Mediterranean streetscape.

Left
F. Pierpont and Walter S. Davis, Roman Gardens, 1926, organizational diagram.

Left, opposite
Franklin Harper, Granada Buildings, 1925. The central courtyard rendered as a virtual street.

Right, opposite
Arthur Larsen, Villa Madrid, 1929. The central courtyard appears to be formed by many buildings on many levels, simulating a Mediterranean hill town street scene.

broken up into two or three substantial terraces by the difference in slope on the site, with each terrace reading as a relatively self-sufficient place. In addition, the buildings surrounding the courtyard are configured such that on their exterior sides, bordering the street, it is not possible to relate them back to the idea of courtyard. Contextual responsiveness distorts the courtyard parti enough to enable us to read it as being larger than a single building.

The six typological categories defined above cover the complete spectrum of court examples observed in southern California. They range from the simplest to the most complex cases of formal definition contained within the confines of a single building type. Courtyard housing arises out of a set of concrete intellectual and pragmatic precedents and develops on the basis of the social and technical expectations and possibilities of southern California up to the beginning of the Second World War. The imagery and organizational principles attached to the typology bespeak its popularity and commercial success as an instrument of urbanization. Its decline and disappearance as a vital element of urban morphology is due to a fundamental shift both in the priorities of production and in the life possibilities associated with the single dwelling in the context of housing.

The Other Housing Tradition

Since the middle of the nineteenth century, the dominant Western intellectual tradition for the design and production of housing has been based on quantitative ideals. An astonishing number of interrelated political, social, economic, and architectural factors have tended to focus attention on the definition of the dwelling unit and its repetition as a measure of validity for all housing prototypes.

Beginning with the early attempts at criticizing the state of the nineteenth-century city and its implicit social structure, critics fixed their attention on the living conditions of the working class. One can identify three different kinds of writing during this period: statements documenting the existing conditions, the verbal or statistical definition of a program for action, and, finally, a variety of concrete financial and building projects for ameliorating the so-called housing problem. In all cases the argument centered on living accommodations as they are embodied in the living unit.

Social scientists, like Engels, or health officials, like Chadwick, were the people who laid the foundations for a public-housing movement in England. Social criticism, which was presented in terms of a socialist ideological framework, described the wretched living quarters of a working class in the process of being exploited by a capitalist minority. The statistical documentation of the existing situation introduced the notion of "standards"—mostly quantitative—that a minimum dwelling had to fulfill. Subsequent descriptions talked repeatedly about numbers of dwellings to be torn down, dwellings to be built, or dwellings to be sanitized. Quantitative standards enforceable by government bodies were seen as the means of remedying the existing situation.

The development of a program for the provision of new housing for the masses was steeped in the egalitarian ideals of the early socialist movements. Repetition of units was seen as a visible, concrete realization of the goal of equal opportunity and equal responsibility for all. During this process, the idea of house, with all its implications of uniqueness, of relationships to the ground, the street, and the public realm, was sacrificed in favor of the neutral term *dwelling unit*. The word *unit* implies statistical, quantitative notions about living and, necessarily, similarity in ways of life among families, whatever their predispositions to different ways of living. The exclusively quantitative nature of the programs was in part based on the awareness of the seriousness of the housing problem and on the conscious decision to ameliorate it as soon as possible for as many people as possible. Early public housing efforts were dominated by the architecturally additive notion of the unit as the building block of the housing scheme. Whether through philanthropist speculation or through public authority, the unit became the instrument of housing financing and production. Here two distinct myths arose concerning the necessity to rationalize housing efforts through the definition of "model" units: first, the production of housing was considered equivalent to the industrial production of other consumer goods. Therefore, the typifying of units was seen as not only efficient in terms of production but also representative of the productive possibilities of an industrializing culture. Second, the efficiently conceived and produced unit became a symbol of living values in the new society. Through living in a "new unit," the working class could not only upgrade its living condition but also reform its habits by aligning its values with those of the developing industrial cultural elites.

In this way the dwelling unit became an instrumental device both in housing production and in the definition of living patterns. And the repetition of units brought about housing projects that represented the formal expression of remedial institutions in a Western society riddled with social conflicts. Starkness and repetition served as reminders of autocratic socialist ideals gone astray in the face of the complexities of behavior of human beings within developing, dynamic social structures.

The Modern movement in the twentieth century received the nineteenth-century housing traditions, accepted them, and amplified them in a number of ways. The idea of a new society that could come about through new building (Le Corbusier: "Architecture *or* Revolution") gave rise to a deterministic notion of a possible tight fit between a reformable proletariat and new types of dwellings. The focus on the ills of the existing city brought about the now notorious efforts (by Le Corbusier, Hilberseimer, and others) to develop new city patterns. The form of housing in the context of urban erasure or suburban development heightened its disconnection from familiar urban patterns and thus from known urban behaviors and instrumental urban memories. Therefore, the remedial social character of housing as a tool of urban re-

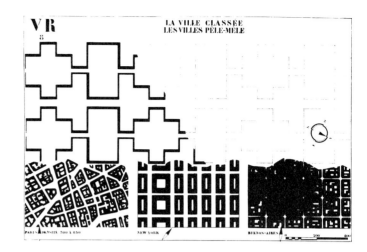

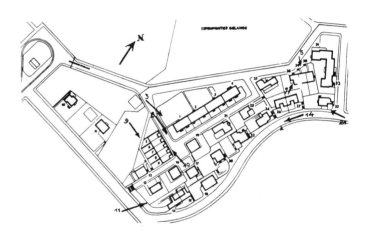

Top
Le Corbusier, diagram from *The Radiant City*, showing the scale of the new Corbusian urban pattern as compared to traditional city structures. This new machine city involved the rejection of traditional building typologies.

Bottom
Weissenhof Housing Settlement, Stuttgart, 1927. Buildings conceived as isolated pieces scattered about the site deny the possibility of coherent urban space or form.

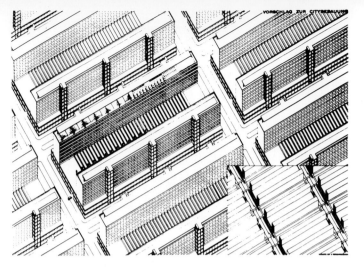

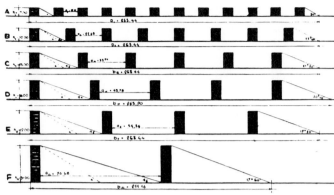

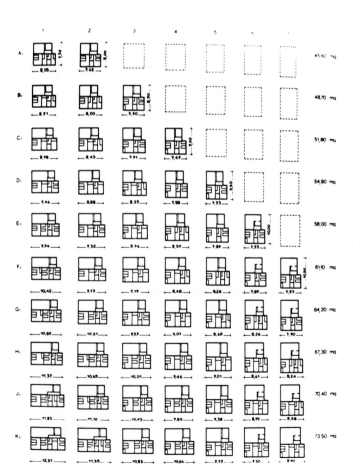

Above left
Ludwig Hilberseimer, axonometric proposal for construction of high-rise buildings, 1927. Hilberseimer, in particular, was an exponent of that popular Germanic notion that equality of accommodation for all inhabitants coupled with machine production would produce the ideal modern city. The resulting repetitious, identical building has become the physical symbol of applied "state-socialist" doctrines.

Above right
Walter Gropius, sectional diagrams of housing at different densities. The ultimate Sachlichkeit deterministic formulas applied to housing.

Left
Alexander Klein, typologies of minimum dwelling, 1929. This is typical of many studies of the 1920s which focused almost exclusively on quantitative variations of the individual dwelling at the expense of any clear notion of overall urban quality or form.

newal was intensified, and a sense of urban alienation was further reinforced. Finally, the pursuit of a machine aesthetic and the rejection of eclectic or vernacular form served to isolate housing from familiar, accessible dwelling symbols. The dwelling unit was expressed architecturally either as an element equivalent to all other units or as a distinct module of production and habitation.

The first housing tradition can then be summarized in the following terms:

1. Typological discontinuity; emphasis on the development of new units aimed at social transformation.
2. Fixation on the singularity of individual dwellings and buildings; their landscape or urban connections are ignored.
3. Pursuit of new egalitarian symbolism based on uniformity and repetition of dwelling unit.
4. Emphasis on economic formulas and machine production as determinants of housing form.
5. Development of programmatic standards that are exclusively quantitative; qualitative concerns based on human experience typically are excluded.

Los Angeles courtyard housing, both as typological structure and as a complete, mature architecture, is suggestive of a second housing paradigm that differs in its fundamental features from the dominant Western housing tradition as outlined before. This "other housing tradition" emphasizes urban continuity and focuses on the development of urban space as a positive element. Buildings are formed as objects that define complex hierarchies of open-air public places at different scales. The shape and content of these places is fixed before issues of individual dwellings are resolved. And in most cases, typological continuity with respect to existing contexts is strictly observed.

In its space rather than mass orientation, housing solutions of the second kind generate a series of public places of definite qualities. First, the street and the service yard are defined either between buildings or by the sharing of common open-space elements among buildings. Typically, the street possesses its own landscape, and it architecturally expresses publicness and formality. The service yard is most often a passage that connects the service areas of each house, and it invariably expresses utility and profanity.

Second, the garage as a place for the storage of machines is always given a prominent and appropriate location in the housing whole. In formal terms it is rendered as a skeletal, minimalist place, and it represents turn-of-the-century notions of formal equivalence between garage and stable.

Finally, the courtyard is a place of contemplation. As a landscape area in unison with the building surfaces that surround it, it is the primary carrier of the implicit meanings of the second housing tradition. The courtyard instructs by association generated through the use of multiple oasis images. It encourages daydreaming in the assignment of social status to the inhabitants, and it represents the possibility of communal motivation within a framework of diversity of accommodation.

The use of landscape, both hard and soft, is so highly developed that the recurring choices of materials and plant life create a familiar environment that modulates the possibilities of physical movement and the flow of light. The concern with the nature of places encompasses the typical Western architectural qualities of the courtyard—light, structure, space; but it also extends into the traditional Middle Eastern qualities of the courts' most distant Arab prototypes— fragrance, acoustic harmony, color, texture. The constituent elements of the architecture of the courtyards include plants, water, and sky. The imagery is potent because it not only reflects a revivalist attitude toward architectures of the past but also seeks clarity in the expression of archetypal architectural relationships and the experiences that these relationships entail.

Indoor and outdoor places are grouped into rooms, and rooms are grouped into dwellings, and dwellings are transformed into courtyard housing in a manner that expresses enormous diversity of accommodation and complexity of space distribution. In radical opposition to the principles of the first housing tradition, a sense of community is achieved through variety and the possibility that disparate architectural elements, when combined, can generate a common public realm.

The second housing tradition is also characterized by an attitude toward building as mass which emphasizes its subtractive possibilities. The reading of buildings as wholes remains more important than the expression of dwellings as increments of production or measures of egalitarian amenity. The element of architectural regularity here is the space of the courtyard rather than the dwelling units of the first housing tradition. The variety and spatial complexity of dwellings is always carried out to the most extreme possibilities. Contextual forces and particular qualities of individual dwellings make each house within a court unique and vital.

Articulations of building mass are carried out for a variety of reasons, often to create extensions to the dwelling or to break up visually the weight of courtyard-enclosing surfaces. Rarely, however—or never, in the case of attached courtyard housing—is the individual dwelling articulated as the important element of the architecture of housing.

Above
Arthur B. Zwebell, the Andalusia,
1926, street edge with parking
courtyard beyond.

Right
Arthur B. Zwebell, the Ronda, 1927,
organizational diagram. Note the
profusion of shaped open places
within the building.

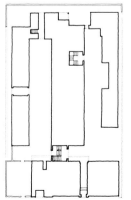

Above
Franklin Harper, Granada Building,
1925. The reading of the building as
a whole is more than the mechanical
articulation of its constituent parts.

The qualities of individual dwellings often border on the lavish, whether in the provision of two-story living rooms, fireplaces, very advanced kitchens and bathrooms, or nicely finished surfaces, or in the possibility of extensions of the dwellings into the surrounding courtyards. The final effects of court living render urban existence bearable in the light of the powerful American suburban ideals. And they overcome the typical disadvantages of suburban living, such as lack of security, a fleeting sense of community, and the absence of public life. It is precisely in its qualities as an alternative to the urban-suburban form dilemma that courts of the second tradition can be considered a valid contemporary housing prototype.

Functionalist notions of space are never utilized. Instead, in the absence of repetition and equivalence of standard building parts, a generalized notion of space prevails. Instead of expressed narrow ideological beliefs, the architecture of the courts symbolizes a whole spectrum of diverse human experiences that are perhaps to be lived in the buildings long after their sponsors and original inhabitants with all their programmatic biases have disappeared.

Within a typically regular parti, dwellings are made unique by being extended out to the courtyard and by being wrapped in a highly expressive, complex wall that invariably communicates messages about the whole building. Movement through the courtyard is rarely afforded its own architecture. The landscape and building elements of the courtyard are strongly individualized, and they are always appropriated by given dwellings. The secret to the maintenance of the publicness of the courts lies in their being surrounded by spaces and walls under private guardianship.

The landscape of the courtyard is conceived as a set of architectural elements, and for that reason its development over time follows a pattern of sophistication through a gradual limitation of means. Usually the ground is subdivided into a regular or symmetrical pattern that is hard paved. The hard paths define parterres that are lined in hedges, either ankle or hip high. In the middle of the intersecting paths is placed an ornate fountain, most often covered in decorative tile. High trees (palms, cypresses, olives) dominate the upper space of each parterre but also allow ample views of the sky. The lower space is filled with a series of chosen species of flower bushes (camellias, azaleas, roses, hibiscus, begonias, bougainvilleas, etc.) or

Below left
Morgan, Walls, and Clements,
Chapman Park Studios, 1928. A
typical maisonette unit, living room.

Below right
Arthur B. Zwebell, the Andalusia,
1926. The exterior building walls on
the courtyard feature elements and
openings at many scales.

Right
Robert Ainsworth, West California
Court, Pasadena, 1927, view of the
courtyard with typical but highly
articulated landscape elements
defining its walls, ground, and
canopy.

various species of palms, philodendron, cactus, and the like. Finally, plants in pots placed on hard surfaces complete the landscape composition of courtyards. The architectural intention is always to make or to suggest place by using plant material to control the ground, the walls, and the canopy of the courtyard and thereby modify the temperature, the sounds and smells, the view, and the physical extensions of each dwelling. In the exteriors of courts, landscape is also utilized to provide a natural envelope around the building which is capable of extension into the city and transformation into an urban element.

The walls that surround courtyards are characterized by a particular set of architectural attitudes. In principle courts do not aim to represent or exude the potential of an industrialized age. They are conceived as forms and sets of places and carried out in the most opportune technology available. The buildings lack a reference to processes of production as ideals. They are dependent on a group of explicit architectural elements—doors, windows, roofs, chimneys, balconies, and the like—and also on a mixed process of handcrafting and machine fabrication which allows constant suggestion and association on the part of the beholder.

The architectural use of these elements makes possible a multiplicity of scale readings in elevation. Typically chimneys, corners, roofs, and entries reflect an urban scale. Thick walls, doors, stairs, windows, porches, balconies, and fountains reflect a building scale. And an extraordinary range of hand-fabricated elements, including tiles, wooden and iron grills, lamps, and canopies, make reference to the scale of components as add ons.

The superposition of scales of surface and landscape is intended to make the courtyard into a vibrant backdrop that induces human experience. The dwelling and the building are lost, and one reads the whole primarily as an urban fragment in the Garden of Eden, expressing the possibilities of individual and communal well-being.

It is difficult to accept the idea of the mature courts as being only revivalist buildings. They can be seen rather as collections of historical parts grafted onto a modern body. If by *nostalgia* we mean the feeling of longing for a place or life lost, then the attempt to recreate places based on a particular contemporary predilection about life past can surely be called nostalgic architecture. The cultural windfall of such a conscious architecture occurs when the nostalgic ambience coincides with the urban, natural, and formal typological traditions of a given context and transforms them to make them appropriate to a given people at a given time.

An emotionally accessible architecture allows the object to become possessed through the limited exposition of known themes, which are presented in part as explicit narrative or place and in part as stimulation to the memory. Furthermore, it allows the city to become accessible and remain familiar by reinforcing its qualities as a backdrop for predictable experience and acceptable risk of change.

The housing of the first tradition represented the efforts of a well-meaning bourgeoisie to resolve issues of dwelling for the working class which did not have their root in form. It began in a complex set of sociopolitical factors that have determined production and consumption in the advanced industrial societies of the last 100 years. As architecture it sponsors new forms to express fabricated goals; it minimizes living potential; and it expresses strife and the irresolvable contradictions of Western society in its current state.

The housing tradition of the second kind was born of the desire to maximize living comfort and experience in the context of a society where dwellings have to be chosen by potential occupants.

The forms utilized to solve the architectural problem of housing address simultaneously issues of city, landscape, and building. In their typological dimension they establish formal and experiential continuity with architectures past. In their stylistic and technical dimension they express narrow, opportunistic meanings relevant specifically to those who made the forms and occupied them. The tremendous ongoing popularity of courts as housing is undoubtedly due to this combined sense of continuity on the one hand and unique response to the culture of southern California on the other.

Below right
Villa Madrid, 1929. Large-scale
elements are in response to the
urban context.

Below left
Villa de la Fuente, 1928.
Middle-scale elements represent the
acceptance of the human body as a
measure of size.

Right
F. Pierpont and Walter S. Davis,
Roman Gardens, 1928. Small-scale
elements are rendered in many
textures that enliven the places with
which the human body is in close
contact.

Case Studies

5 Within the typological diversity of Los Angeles courtyard housing taken as a whole, individual examples offer complete and accomplished architectural solutions. The following catalog of outstanding courts is offered in the hope that they will illustrate the potential transformation of buildings from parti to constructed object, a process that includes adherence to abstract typological rules, the development of appropriate imagery, and the generation of places that enhance human life.

Richard Requa's foreword to *Architectural Details: Spain and the Mediterranean* offers the most extensive prescription available of how these basic conditions of all great design could be accommodated within the urban and design confines of a Spanish Revival architecture. It is a text that inspired a generation of architects and provided the specific impulses for the twenty-eight case studies that follow:

There is perhaps no section of the world of greater interest to Californians than Spain and the countries bordering the western Mediterranean.

This is due first to the fact that the greater portion of southwestern America was discovered, explored and settled by adventurers and missionaries from southern Spain. The picturesque old missions and other interesting structures built by them along the Pacific slopes, and evidencing their endeavors, devotion and struggles, are reminiscent of the beautiful buildings of their home land.

Then, the climate, topography and other natural conditions found in southern Europe and north Africa are strikingly similar to conditions found in the southwest section of our own country. Indeed, in traveling along the Mediterranean littoral, one is constantly reminded of Southern California; the same general aspect of the landscape, the same character of wild growth, the same soft colorings and the same balmy, congenial atmosphere. The roadways are frequently bordered with eucalyptus and palms; the hillsides are dotted with citrus orchards, olive groves and vineyards; and the parks, plazas and patios are filled with the same trees, shrubs, vines and flowering plants, growing in the same luxuriance and profusion as in Southern California.

But undoubtedly the main reason for the rapidly increasing interest in the western Mediterranean countries is the growing appreciation of the fact that the logical, fitting and altogether appropriate architecture for California and the Pacific southwest is a style inspired and suggested by the architecture of those countries.

The fundamental characteristics of the architecture of all the western Mediterranean countries are substantially the same.

The walls of the buildings were built of rough masonry finished on the exterior with stucco, whitewashed or tinted in light pastel shades harmonizing with the landscape.

The roofs were either constructed flat or low-pitched, covered with red, burned clay tiles.

Ornament was used with great restraint and discrimination, and not without definite reason and purpose. It usually consisted of simple, well designed mouldings, corbels, brackets, pilasters and columns, concentrated and disposed so as to leave generous areas of plain wall surfaces.

Exterior interest, attractiveness and charm was obtained rather by wrought iron, wood or stuccoed window grilles, shutters, balconies or other similar practical features.

The focal point of the exterior design was usually the main entrance, the doors of which were sometimes elaborately paneled and ornamented with wrought iron hardware, studs and bolt heads of beautiful pattern.

Courts, patios and gardens were quite an indispensable feature of the architectural treatment. These were made intimate with the buildings by means of colonnades, arcades, loggias, and paved terraces. The garden areas were made inviting and gay with fountains, pools, pergolas, polychrome tile seats, exedras and other interesting garden accessories. Flowering plants in terra cotta pots were also used profusely in the gardens, on the parapets and covering the balconies.

Through centuries of development, the foregoing basic features have been found most essential and harmonious in the design of buildings for an environment such as exists in California; therefore, it is reasonable to presume they are the fundamental characteristics of the logical architectural style for the Pacific southwest.

The author endeavored, in his recent trip through the Mediterranean countries, to photograph such details of their buildings and gardens as could be appropriately used, or at least serve as inspiration, for developing the California style.

From some six hundred negatives he made in southern Europe, north Africa and the islands of the Mediterranean, such details were selected for this work as would, in his opinion, be of the greatest interest and value to California architects, and these have been classified and arranged to facilitate their use in the drafting room.[1]

The Zwebell Courts

Arthur and Nina Zwebell gave Los Angeles a unique building heritage in a burst of activity that lasted less than a decade. During the 1920s, this team designed and built several single-family houses, but their fame will, without doubt, rest on eight or so buildings of a character peculiar to Los Angeles which we have termed "courtyard housing."

Beginnings

Arthur Zwebell and Nina Wilcox Zwebell grew up in the Midwest. She was an avid musician and graduated from Northwestern University in 1914. He was a self-educated man—his formal education did not go beyond the eighth grade. His talents for invention and design became apparent early in life through his first great passion, automobiles. Not only did he invent a version of the tire vulcanizer, but he designed and produced a sporty roadster body to be attached to standard Ford chassis.

Three years after their marriage in 1914, the Zwebells traveled to Los Angeles while on vacation and returned in 1921 to live there permanently. They brought with them $35,000 and the desire to build.

The Designer-Builders

Arthur Zwebell immediately found himself a contractor. With the assistance of Nina, who created all the interiors, he designed and developed his first court, a Norman-style building, now destroyed, called Quaint Village.

Arthur learned quickly. He proceeded to design and build a number of single-family houses. In 1922–1923, his second court appeared in Hollywood in an astonishing Hansel-and-Gretel fantasy style. Meanwhile, Nina established an interiors firm as well as a furniture factory, where she concurrently designed and produced period furniture throughout the 1920s. The Zwebells never operated an office as such but preferred to work out of their own house. Most architectural and design drawings were executed by them, with occasional outside help. Architects and engineers were hired merely to sign necessary drawings.

Above left
Arthur and Nina Zwebell with their
son Robert, circa 1920.

Left
Arthur Zwebell, circa 1950.

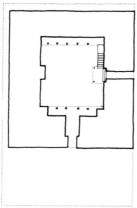

Above
Villa Primavera, 1923, entrance from
Harper Avenue.

Left
Villa Primavera, 1923, organizational
diagram.

The Villa Primavera

West Hollywood, 1923

The Zwebells' first known exceptional courtyard housing experiment was the Villa Primavera (also referred to as the Mexican Village). It was situated in a part of Hollywood where in 1923 only one other house existed. The change in style to Spanish Revival in this work and in subsequent projects executed in the 1920s seems to be more a response to popular demand than a doctrinaire architectural attachment to Mediterranean forms.

For the first time we can see the essential ingredients of the developer courtyard housing type. The Spanish-style wood-and-stucco structure completely surrounds a courtyard that is animated by a tiled fountain, outside fireplace, and lush foliage. Parking is cleverly integrated into the overall design, in this case by incorporation into one side of the building mass. All ten housing units have their primary access and existence dependent upon the court. Interior zoning capitalizes on views of the central space. Services are typically placed on exterior walls and away from the courtyard itself.

The Villa Primavera is located on a corner site with major entrance set back and minor entrance flush to the street. Its rambling appearance belies a plan configuration that is nearly a perfect square. Everything but the two-story east wing is on one level. The living units on this side are miniature in scale but still possess a certain charm—each has a corner fireplace, small niches, exposed timber ceiling, and tiled floors. The dwellings on the other sides are somewhat larger and much more spatially complex—harbingers of the Zwebells' later development.

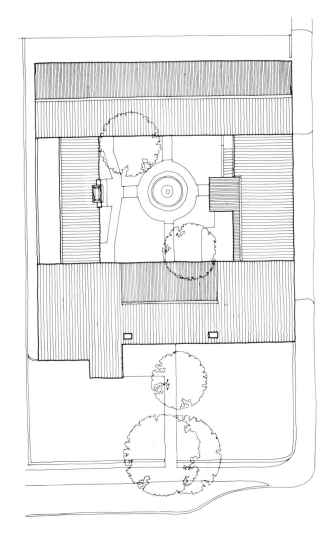

Above
Villa Primavera, 1923, roof plan.

Above
Villa Primavera, 1923, view of
courtyard with fountain and
fireplace.

Left
Villa Primavera, 1923, section.

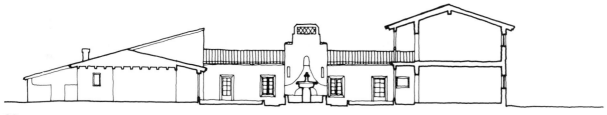

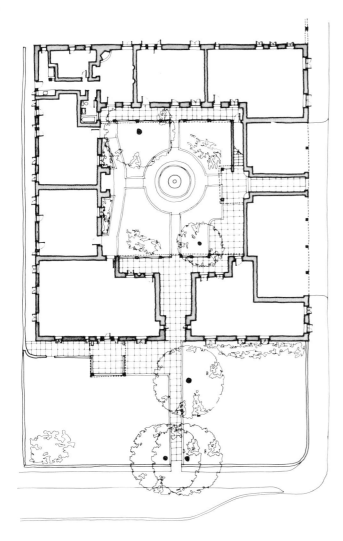

Above
Villa Primavera, 1923, ground-floor
plan.

Above right
Villa Primavera, 1923, detail of
fountain.

Below right
Villa Primavera, 1923, richly
landscaped courtyard as seen from
upper loggia.

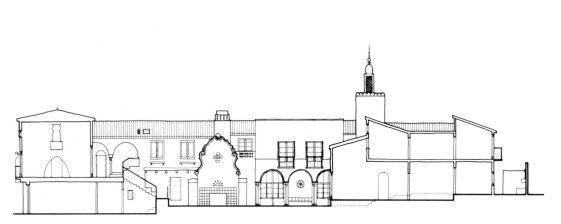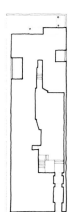

The Patio del Moro
West Hollywood, 1925

After the completion of Villa Primavera, where the Zwebells themselves resided, a number of commissions quickly followed, including several houses in Pasadena and one for Harold Lloyd's mother next to the actor's estate in Beverly Hills. Then the Zwebells used the subdivided plot of the Primavera as the site for their next courtyard-housing experiment, the Patio del Moro.

While most of the Zwebells' buildings are modeled after pure Andalusian prototypes, the Patio del Moro displays a clear influence of Arab form sources: pointed and horseshoe arches, surface arabesque patterns, latticed openings, and countless other details. In fact, the specific stylistic tendencies in the design of the building were imposed by the client, a physician who had traveled widely in North Africa and Spain and had strong preferences for Moorish motifs.

The Patio del Moro is a compact U-shaped building in plan. It makes a definite wall on the street, where garages and an arched main entrance are located. The enclosed courtyard contains lush landscape elements, including a delicate reflecting pool and a robust baroque fireplace. The beautiful tile work and an exotic Tunisian tower complete the ensemble.

All seven units within the Patio del Moro use the court as a kind of vestibule. In addition, each dwelling has a private terrace, patio, or balcony, suggesting a careful gradation of public to private outdoor space. The dwellings display a great deal of spatial complexity, as two-story living spaces and mezzanines dominate the interior design.

The impression of variety in the dwelling demonstrates Arthur Zwebell's virtuosity in mainipulating standardized elements so that individual identity results. For example, some dwellings are essentially mirror images, yet they are perceived as quite different from one another because of their unexpected placement in the building configuration.

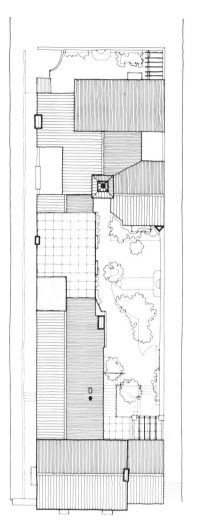

Above
Patio del Moro, 1925, roof plan.

Above, opposite
Patio del Moro, 1925, Fountain
Avenue facade.

Below left, opposite
Patio del Moro, 1925, section.

Below right, opposite
Patio del Moro, 1925, organizational
diagram.

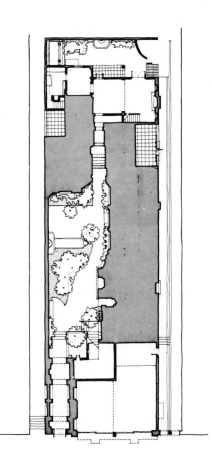

Left
Patio del Moro, 1925, detail of
ornamental treatment of front facade.

Below left
Patio del Moro, 1925, vehicular and
pedestrian entrances.

Below
Patio del Moro, 1925, ground-floor
plan.

Below
Patio del Moro, 1925, view of
baroque fireplace and pigeon tower
in courtyard.

Below
Patio del Moro, 1925, detail of entry
passage.

Below
Patio del Moro, 1925, living room
view from dining room in rear unit.

Below
Patio del Moro, 1925, rear unit living
room with sleeping loft above.

Below
Patio del Moro, 1925, living room with
sleeping loft above in unit above
entry.

Below
Patio del Moro, 1925, living room with
peacock fireplace in unit above
entry.

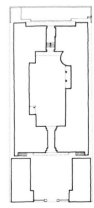

The Andalusia

West Hollywood, 1926

In 1926, the Zwebells sold the Villa Primavera in order to develop their next court, the Andalusia. This extraordinary building firmly established their reputation. By now, Arthur Zwebell had mastered a daring and pure Andalusian style and was supported by an array of craftsmen. Perhaps the Zwebells' most accomplished building, the Andalusia incorporates the best features of all the experiments. Its overall form and the dwelling pieces are beautifully resolved.

In the Andalusia, the problem of parking has been ingeniously worked out. The garages, if they may be called that, are actually two pavilions, one flanking each side of a forecourt. The impression one gets is of three separate but exquisitely related outdoor rooms: one off the street and paved, reserved primarily for the automobile; the second, within the body of the court, rendered as an Andalusian patio and directly related to the nine dwellings; and the third, located in the most private part of the site, also finished in hard materials and reserved for recreational activities. The small archways cut into the body of the building heighten the sensation of spatial connection.

The units continue the spatial experiments of the Patio del Moro, culminating in the Zwebells' own dwelling: within is an extraordinarily beautiful two-story living space that was designed specifically to accommodate a pipe organ for Nina Zwebell.

The Andalusia was (and continues to be) a favorite watering place for aspiring and established members of the motion picture set. Some of the more famous past residents of the Andalusia include Clara Bow, Jean Hagen, John Payne, Cesar Romero, and Teresa Wright.[2]

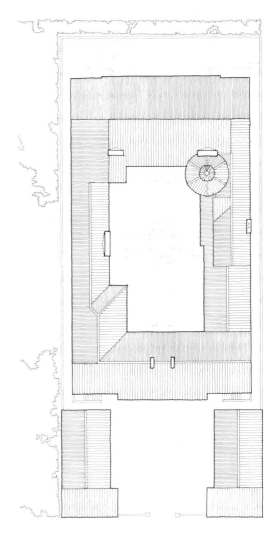

Above
The Andalusia, 1926, roof plan.

Above, opposite
The Andalusia, 1926, entrance forecourt with flanking garages.

Below left, opposite
The Andalusia, 1926, section.

Below right, opposite
The Andalusia, 1926, organizational diagram.

Left
The Andalusia, 1926, photograph of forecourt taken in 1927.

Below left
The Andalusia, 1926, view of central courtyard shortly after completion of construction, 1927.

Below right
The Andalusia, 1926, ground-floor plan.

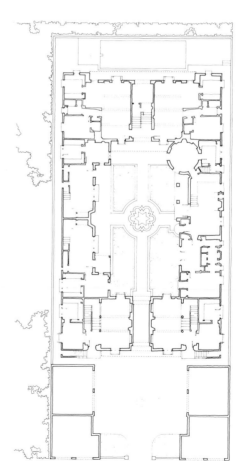

Left
The Andalusia, 1926, detail of entrance gate.

Below left
The Andalusia, 1926, entrance forecourt seen from street with central courtyard beyond.

Below right
The Andalusia, 1926, tiled stairs to upper-level front units.

Left
The Andalusia, 1926, raised pool in rear patio.

Below left
The Andalusia, 1926, view of central courtyard.

Below right
The Andalusia, 1926, detail of fountain and fireplace in courtyard.

Left
The Andalusia, 1926, Zwebell
maisonette living room.

Below left
The Andalusia, 1926, Zwebell
maisonette living room seen from
organ loft.

Below right
At the Andalusia, Bernice Clair,
promotional photograph of an
aspiring movie star, circa 1927.

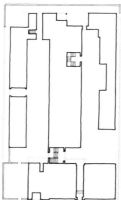

Above
The Ronda, 1927, west facade shortly after completion of construction.

Left
The Ronda, 1927, organizational diagram.

The Ronda

West Hollywood, 1927

In 1927, the Zwebells acquired the land where they were to build their next major work, christened the Ronda. The Ronda's plan configuration is unique in the Zwebell oeuvre. The single centralized court has been abandoned in favor of two linear spaces that from certain vantage points appear to be picturesque Andalusian streets. Certainly the large size of the lot — about twice that of the Andalusia — influenced this solution.

The Ronda contains twenty units. Set directly against the street on the west is a continuous wall of dwellings that step from four stories to two, with three lower apartment blocks running at a perpendicular angle. In between these building blocks, and at different levels, are some of the most wonderful exterior spaces to be found in Los Angeles.

There are a great variety of dwellings in the Ronda, including cottages, maisonettes with two-story spaces and mezzanines, and some interesting split-level units. These last were the result of Arthur Zwebell's clever accommodation of the half-sunken basement garage to the north and the lower court to the south. Typically, he turned a knotty problem into an ingenious solution.

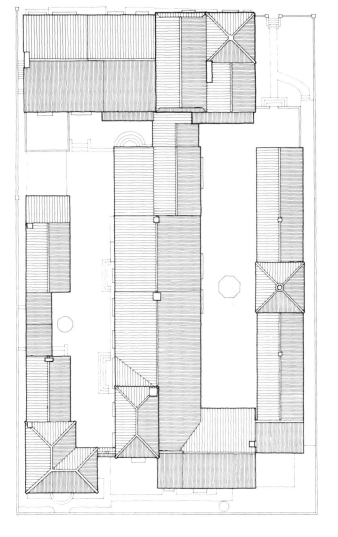

Above
The Ronda, 1927, roof plan.

Above
The Ronda, 1927, south garden
courtyard, general view.

Right
The Ronda, 1927, ground-floor plan.

Below right
The Ronda, 1927, section.

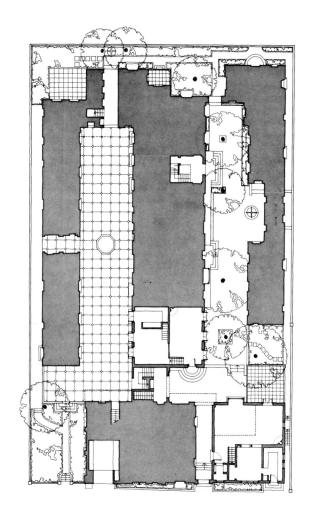

85

Left
The Ronda, 1927, north tiled patio.

Left
The Ronda, 1927, south garden
courtyard, sitting room.

Below right
The Ronda, 1927, south garden courtyard, The Chapel.

Below left
The Ronda, 1927, entrance patio.

Left
The Ronda, 1927, entrance patio with arched access to parking garage.

Below right
The Ronda, 1927, typical living room.

Below left
The Ronda, 1927, view of split-level
dining/living room.

Right
The Ronda, 1927, living room with
access to south garden.

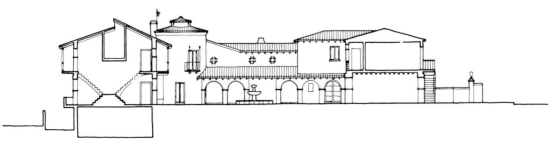

90

El Cabrillo

Hollywood, 1928

A year later, the Zwebells moved their building activity eastward, first designing El Cabrillo in Hollywood and then the Casa Laguna in Los Feliz. El Cabrillo appears to be a judicious attempt to duplicate the Andalusia at a different site and in a different material. The massing of the two buildings is identical. As a corner building, however, El Cabrillo was originally entered from both streets. Unfortunately, because of continual street widening, the main entry has been closed altogether, and the building configuration on the sidewalk has been considerably altered.

El Cabrillo is not built in wood and stucco, as are virtually all the other Zwebell courts. Instead, a concrete block, nonstandard in size, is used in an apparent attempt to create an adobe-block effect. The ten units follow the Zwebell pattern of incorporating two-story living rooms, mezzanines, and graceful staircases. All the dwelling interiors are skillfully modeled in light with a variety of window openings. Especially effective are small lunette windows in the upper part of the living-room space.

El Cabrillo was intended as a place of residence for both transient and permanent members of the Hollywood scene. One of the Talmadge sisters lived here, Hollywood lore connects the name of Cecil B. De Mille's daughter with this building, and at least one of Rudolph Valentino's films is alleged to have used El Cabrillo as a stage set.

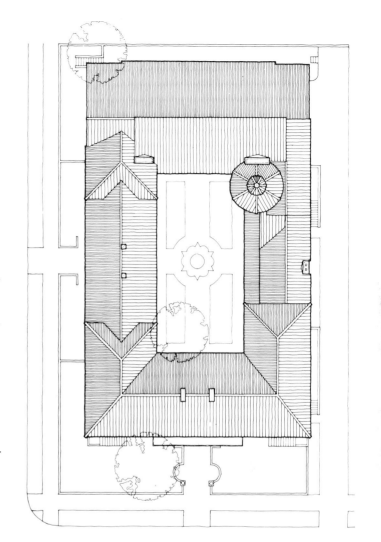

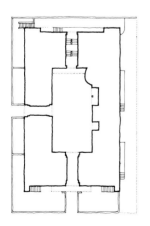

Below left
El Cabrillo, 1928, organizational diagram.

Above
El Cabrillo, 1928, roof plan.

Below, opposite
El Cabrillo, 1928, section.

Above, opposite
El Cabrillo, 1928, aerial view.

Left
El Cabrillo, 1928, view of the arcaded
south wall of the courtyard.

Below left
El Cabrillo, 1928, central courtyard
with fountain and turret.

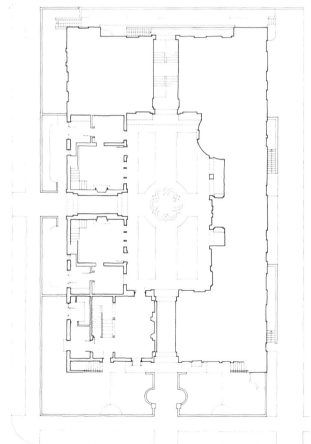

Below
El Cabrillo, 1928, ground-floor plan.

Left
El Cabrillo, 1928, west facade with walled private patios.

Below left
El Cabrillo, 1928, entrance gate with passage and fountain beyond.

Below
El Cabrillo, 1928, upper loggia and
passage on the west facade of the
courtyard.

Left
El Cabrillo, 1928, passageway to
Franklin Avenue with baroque
window and flanking chimneys
above.

Below left
El Cabrillo, 1928. A typical
double-volume living room.

Below
El Cabrillo, 1928, upper balcony and
stairway with view into sleeping
rooms above.

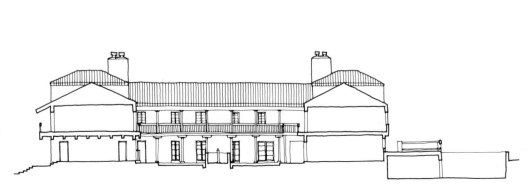

The Casa Laguna

Los Feliz, 1928

Like the Primavera and El Cabrillo, the Casa Laguna is located on a corner site. Its major entrance is set back considerably from the street, recalling a similar solution in the Primavera. Secondary pedestrian and vehicular access through separate entries occurs on the adjacent side. The automobile entry pierces through an extension of the main building to a lower paved court and a row of garages located beneath a communal sun terrace.

The square courtyard contains the usual Zwebell features. What makes it special is its generous proportions for the twelve surrounding units. In addition, there is an elaborate two-story loggia with intricate wooden capitals and stone columns reminiscent of such Andalusian prototypes as the Casa del Chapiz in Granada.

The underplayed exterior of the Casa Laguna belies unusual and complex interiors. The additional terrace on the west allows the units in this building a more varied and open exposure than in the earlier courts.

After the Courts

In 1929, with the complete collapse of the private housing market, the Zwebells turned to other occupations. They were first engaged as set designers in the movie studios, later turning to furniture design and production.

Arthur made an abortive attempt to return to building with a plan to manufacture a modular housing system in 1934–1936. Unfortunately for Zwebell and the history of architecture in Los Angeles, he had to rely on sponsorship of the Federal Housing Authority during that economically troubled era. Even though his efforts proceeded to the point where he designed and built a prototype house, relations with the housing authorities were so difficult and bitter that after a storm damaged his housing plant in Van Nuys, he took his insurance settlement and quit building.

Except for three residences for his family in North Hollywood, Arthur Zwebell never practiced architecture again. He died in 1973. Nina Wilcox Zwebell died the next year.

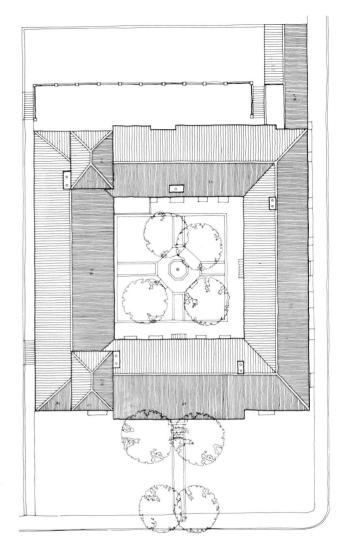

Above
Casa Laguna, 1928, roof plan.

Above, opposite
Casa Laguna, 1928, central courtyard with fountain and fireplace.

Below left, opposite
Casa Laguna, 1928, section.

Below right, opposite
Casa Laguna, 1928, organizational diagram.

Below
Casa Laguna, 1928, main entrance.

Below
Casa Laguna, 1928, ground-floor
plan.

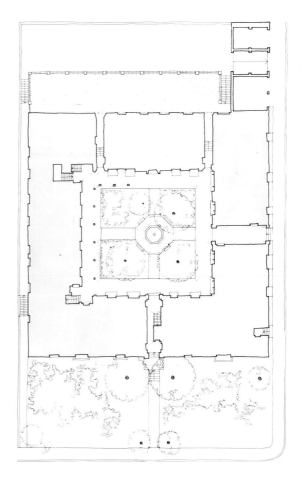

Left
Casa Laguna, 1928, parking court
with elevated terrace above.

Below left
Arcade with wooden
balcony above.

Below right
Casa Laguna, 1928, detail of
courtyard wall.

The Zwebells' Contribution

Without doubt, Arthur and Nina Zwebell were the originators of the highly refined deluxe court in Los Angeles. However brief an interlude theirs was in the building history of the region, their contribution is extraordinary, with their concern for traditional urban form, their adaptation and development of the southern California court type of housing, their use of landscape as a discrete formal language, and the richness of the individual units in each court.

Both Zwebells were consciously opposed to the forms of modern architecture and design. They were "ancients" in the sense that they sought inspiration in the imagery of the past. This, however, is only part of their story, for, paradoxically, Arthur demanded and finally achieved an architecture that in a planning sense was as rational as any truly modern work was supposed to be. We have only to consider the variety of ingenious parking solutions he generated to dismiss once and for all any temptation to view this work as that of a dilettante. This duality is evident in both Zwebell's devotion to the Spanish Mediterranean style and his audacious attempt at factory-produced housing.

The Zwebells' complete control of their projects, from finance to construction, and their unique combination of business and design skills generated a set of exemplary buildings that served as a standard for most examples of courtyard housing that followed. From our perspective today, their work is valid as more than just a model for future housing experiments; it is also, in absolute terms, architecture of the highest quality—some of the finest ever created in Los Angeles.

Right
The five Davis children, circa 1922.
From left to right: standing, Pierpont, Emmett; *sitting,* Henry, Walter S., Dorothy.

Opposite
Cover design from *Ideal Homes in Garden Communities* by Walter S. Davis et al., 1916.

100

The Davis Courts

F. Pierpont and Walter S. Davis designed several of the most distinguished of the courtyard apartments of Los Angeles. Unlike the Zwebells, who combined a midwestern pragmatism with a keen eye for Spanish architectural detail, the Davises were established architects embedded in the ways of the academy.

Like many in their profession during the 1920s, they were facile but conservative interpreters of various historical styles that included both the highly established classical modes of the Italian and French Renaissance and the vernacular forms of rural Italy and Spain. They were also capable of improvising across visual traditions. Their mixing of Italian and Spanish-Moorish images into strange Mediterranean concoctions produced buildings that are not only nostalgic and recollective but also new and bizarre— inventive permutations without direct historical precedent.

Background

The Davis brothers were sons of Henry Davis, a Baltimore architect. Pierpont (1884–1953) arrived in Los Angeles in 1905 after having apprenticed with his father. Walter S. (1887–1973) studied architecture at the Massachusetts Institute of Technology and graduated in 1911. He had first visited Europe in 1905, after high school; in 1911–1912 he returned to the Continent as a recipient of an MIT traveling scholarship. His ship landed in Algeciras; from there he journeyed to Ronda, Seville, Granada, and Cordoba; during this trip he also visited France and Italy. In 1912 he joined his brother in Los Angeles.

California Garden City Homes

Shortly after his arrival, Walter S. Davis coauthored a book o standard building types appropriate to California with the help of his brother Henry, a landscape architect, H. Scott Gerity, and Loyall F. Watson. *California Garden City Homes,* published in 1915, contains the seed of the most important architectural ideas that the firm of F. Pierpont and Walter S. Davis realized in the brief years of its existence. Subsequent editions included finished Davis buildings in place of

previously proposed designs. The following excerpt, a discussion of the patio, constitutes an early call for the development of a Mediterranean architecture in southern California. It also describes the romantic sources and therefore the evocative qualities of this brand of revivalism. The design of the Davis courts, although removed in time from their writings, nonetheless represented a direct expression of the building and life ideals expressed in the text:

There are many types of homes but none appeal to Californians more than the patio. In fact the world over in countries noted for the salubrity of their climate, the profusion of their foliage and flowers, the brightness of their sunshine and the blueness of their sky, the plan of a house with its living and sleeping rooms grouped around a central court is the one most in favor. The preference for this arrangement is not a fancy of the moment; rather it is the result of centuries of experience in house planning. Spain, Italy, Greece, alike noted for their civilizations and their development of architecture, have all favored the patio plan.

When one thinks of the home of an ancient Roman, he immediately recalls the houses of Pompeii. The front on the narrow street was ignored; the houses presented walls unbroken by any opening except the doors. Entering the dark shadowed doorway and pushing aside the heavy curtains one stepped out into a court, beautiful and brilliant. Green grass, gorgeous flowers, marble columns and the red tiled roof sparkled in the sunlight and were reflected in the lily pool in the center with an intensity even more vivid than the actuality. Above and far off smoked purple Vesuvius, and through a columned portico, the Bay of Naples curved to the shores of Baiae [sic], a dark sea of lapis lazuli.

Similar in arrangement to the Pompeiian houses were the homes of the Moors, the Kings of Granada. For a scene of Oriental luxury, a vision of fairyland splendor, the courts of the Alhambra would serve well. The long, cool pools still reflect, as they did centuries ago, the soft, yellow stucco of the walls, the brilliant green and blue faience and the bejewelled pattern work of the ornament. Every now and then, with a swirl of gold, a fish rising to the surface sends the reflections coiling and twisting into the cool, green shadows of the orange and the pomegranate. Coming from the glare of the Spanish sun into the quiet and cool of the courts, one is immediately refreshed and filled with the restful charm of these beautiful patios.

With memories of the Alhambra and of their own homes fresh in their minds, the Spanish Dons who settled California built their new houses around cool, beflowered patios. Today several examples still remain; the cloisters of Santa Barbara and Ramona's home at San Diego. Who has not, charmed with the beauty of these patios, thought to himself, "I, too, will have a home like this!"[3]

Partnership

In 1918, during World War I, Walter S. Davis found himself in Europe with the American armed forces. In 1919, after his return to Los Angeles, the two brothers embarked upon the development of a speculative house that eventually and over the next five years mushroomed into their first elaborate courtyard housing building. Called the French Village, it was located on Highland Avenue at the entrance to Cahuenga Pass. The architects' own office was built in the mid-twenties as a mixed-use court on the corner of 6th and New Hampshire streets in Los Angeles. In the early twenties the Davises joined a group called Allied Architects, which was formed to share public work as it became available through the city of Los Angeles.

In 1926 and then in 1928 they designed and developed the Villa d'Este and the Roman Gardens, two of the most lavish courts in the city. The two buildings are most accomplished as architecture and served as a substantial source of income. While Pierpont became wealthy through marriage, Walter S. used this income as a way to reaffirm his commitment to a highly sensitive eclecticism based primarily on French and Italian and secondarily on Spanish models. Important 1920s commissions included the Kappa Delta Phi sorority house at the University of California, Los Angeles, and Saint John's Episcopal Church and Patriotic Hall in downtown Los Angeles.

Left
Italian garden watercolor by Walter
S. Davis. (circa 1929)

Opposite
The Roman Gardens, 1926, roof
plan.

Below
The Roman Gardens, 1926, section.

Above
The Roman Gardens, 1926. The
court is nestled in the Hollywood
Hills.

The Roman Gardens

Hollywood, 1926

The Roman Gardens is one of the most sumptuous courts in Los Angeles. Within its fantastic ambience the Davises have combined images from Italy, Spain, and North Africa, creating perhaps the most romantic courtyard buildings to be found in Los Angeles.

Although originally the building was called Roman Gardens, for years it has been referred to as the Villa Valentino because of the insistent popular legend that Rudolph Valentino used it as the center of his amorous activities. The Roman Gardens is nestled picturesquely at the base of a hill across from the Hollywood Bowl. It is ensconced in exotic foliage, a mixture of eucalyptus, jasmine, palm, jacaranda, citrus trees, oleander, and Italian pine which is typical of the older developed areas of the Hollywood Hills.

The building is set well back from busy Highland Avenue. It is entered through a now paved and generously planted forecourt space. A side service drive that serves both the Roman Gardens and the adjacent building to the north gives access to the parking area with entrances either into the side of the garden forecourt or into one of the rear entrances of the villa. Along this side there was originally a garage that opened to the alley and made a wall for the north side of the entrance garden.

The basic axial, symmetrical order of the garden approach is offset by the asymmetrically positioned tower on the north. This tower, a curious spire of Spanish-Moorish origins, dominates the approach and gives clues to the asymmetrical arrangement inside. Indeed, the building, once one is past the exterior gardens and formal entrance, loses any image of formal consistency and appears almost as a cluster of different structures loosely grouped around several courtyard spaces.

One moves through a total of three courts that alternate from left to right. The first of these, hard paved, functions simultaneously as a vestibule and as a focus for surrounding living units. The middle court, lined with mature trees and discreetly placed terraces, is obviously the intended focus of the complex. In the last court, diminutive in scale, a lovely fountain and irregular surfaces create a third type of space, one that is both informal and intimate.

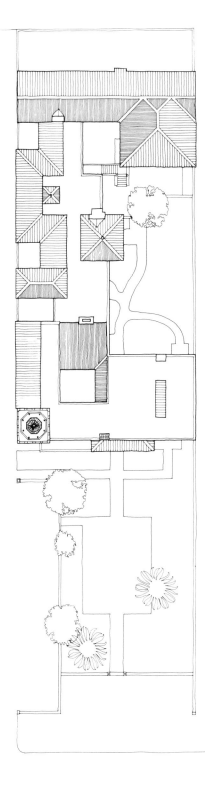

The apartments themselves are a strange mix of hybrid types. Some are two-story maisonettes with private entrances but opening from a two-story-high living room directly to the semiprivate space of the interior courts. Some units cluster around the small rear paved court and have access to this space. Several apartments have private patios to the north, each with a beautiful tile and stucco fountain with water rushing from the mouth of a lion or a fantastic creature of mythical or medieval origin.

Other apartments have access from a variety of stairs, some of which are tiled or equipped with fragments of past or imagined buildings, including Corinthian columns, medallions, and parts of stone lions. Some upper apartments are huge two-story-high spaces with elaborate exposed timber ceilings.

It is this curious combination of the random and unique interiors and courtyards and the formally coherent exterior that gives the Roman Gardens much of its charm. The repetitive monotony of the typical apartment structure has nowhere been more marvelously disguised or picturesquely sited, and the building is a special jewel, a virtual cinematographic stage set without equal or precedent.

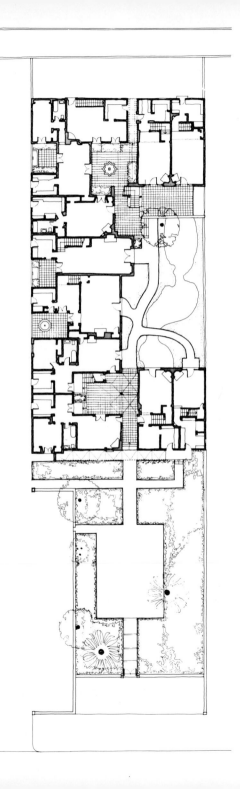

Above, opposite
The Roman Gardens, 1926,
organizational diagram.

Right
The Roman Gardens, 1926,
ground-floor plan.

Below left
The Roman Gardens, 1926, main
entrance.

Below right
The Roman Gardens, 1926, arcade
with central courtyard beyond.

Left
The Roman Gardens, 1926, central courtyard seen from beyond the south wall.

Below left
The Roman Gardens, 1926, view of central courtyard, circa 1950.

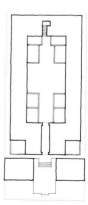

The Villa d'Este

West Hollywood, 1928

The Villa d'Este, despite the borrowing of the name, bears little architectural resemblance to its namesake in Tivoli. It is rather the unique design of fountains, pools, and connecting waterways which allows us to understand the appropriateness of the name.

The court contains diverse stylistic elements mixed to form a stable, almost stiff, building symmetrically disposed along its entrance axis. This is perhaps the most sober of the Davis courts. Its Italian Renaissance exterior was inspired by the Italian villas depicted in the many copybooks that adorned the shelves of all serious eclectic architects of the 1920s, especially the villas of rural Tuscany. The building is also a reflection of the formal preferences of Walter S. Davis, who in his wonderful watercolor paintings has captured the intensity of the Italian countryside and its buildings. The interior of the court is an assemblage of mostly Italian vernacular elements but, again, symmetrically arranged to reinforce a sense of formality and to exaggerate the building's weight.

The basic parti of the Villa d'Este strongly resembles Arthur Zwebell's Andalusia in the accommodation of garages on the street. Not only did the Davises create a wonderful parking forecourt next to the sidewalk, but tandem parking inside the garages allows unusually high unit-to-car ratios. Entrance into the court happens through an elevated platform between the garages.

Without doubt the most extraordinary feature of the Villa d'Este is the landscape of its central courtyard. Each unit is given a walled private garden, and they all share a central major place, dominated by a fountain. Water emerges from the mouth of a lion mounted on a column, a copy from the Palazzo Bevilacqua in Bologna. It then runs into a groove in the paving, around the fountain, down the steps, and into the ground, in a manner similar to the gardens of the Alhambra in Granada. Finally, the water issues forth again from the mouth of yet another lion, which dominates a pond on the entrance steps of the villa. The sound, visual presence, and coolness of the water provide a vital dimension to the courtyard.

There is limited plasticity in the development of the building masses enclosing the courtyard. Selected fragments of

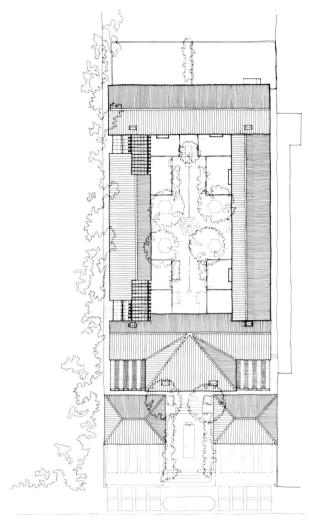

Above
Villa d'Este, 1928, roof plan.

Above, opposite
Villa d'Este, 1928, entry facade with parking forecourt.

Below left, opposite
Villa d'Este, 1928, section.

Below right, opposite
Villa d'Este, 1928, organizational diagram.

these masses were developed by Walter S. Davis for his early stock houses. Especially interesting in the Villa d'Este is the derivation of its second-story roof garden from House Number 57, of 1915. The overall choice and treatment of stylistic surface fragments is timid and safe.

The apartments offer diverse accommodations with especially generous public rooms related to the central courtyard. The Davises were particularly fond of taking care of such modern details as kitchens and bathrooms in their courts, and this court is no exception. Although the Villa d'Este does not offer the uniqueness of dwelling types found in the Roman Gardens, it is nonetheless a building of very high dwelling standards.

Despite the charm of its apartments, the compositional qualities of its plan, and its stylistic fragments, the genius of this building lies in the subtle upward sequence of public places from the street to the semiprivate stairs at the end of the courtyard. Its enduring popularity and quality are a living testament to the insight of the Davis brothers.

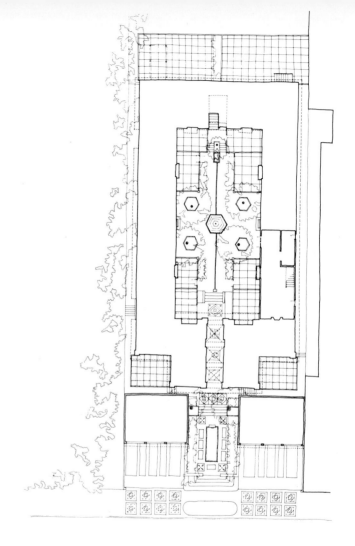

Above
Villa d'Este, 1928, ground-floor plan.

Opposite
Villa d'Este, 1928, entrance with reflecting pool.

Below left
Villa d'Este, 1928, central courtyard
with fountain.

Below right
Villa d'Este, 1928, detail of lion
fountain, a copy from Palazzo
Bevilacqua, Bologna, Italy.

Left
Villa d'Este, 1928, private walled patios within the central courtyard.

Below left
Villa d'Este, 1928, elaborately paved passage seen from inside the courtyard.

Below right
Villa d'Este, 1928, view from rear of courtyard showing the water fountain and channels.

The El Greco Apartments

Westwood, 1929

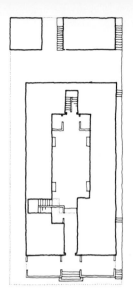

The El Greco Apartments were designed by Pierpont at the end of the partnership between the two brothers, while Walter S. was living with his family in Rome. Without a doubt, this court does not live up to the quality of the other two produced by the same office. One reason has to do with the diminutive site, which forced the architect to shrink the units and the courtyard space to miniature, almost unacceptable dimensions. In addition, the relegation of parking to the back of the building creates a zone of car-dominated territory around it which is not given a significant architectural definition.

The most prominent aspect of the building is its public entrance on the street. The doorway is overscaled; the Italian country villa detail is sparse and almost disappears under the concerted attacks of ivy. Two private walled patios form a transition from the street to the entrance which, along with the steps on the ground, helps establish the place of entry decisively.

The courtyard is strangely empty, possibly because of neglect or redesign, but the scale of the buildings that surround it is both agreeably urban and decidedly Spanish. No scalar urban plays are at work here, but the detail is crisp and the imagery convincing.

The individual apartments are small but extremely efficient and thoughtfully planned. They illustrate how a sensitive architect can operate within seriously delimited boundaries. Individual units do not offer the extraordinary configurations of other courts.

Although the El Greco Apartments do not offer the stability and formality of the Villa d'Este or the asymmetry and variety of the Roman Gardens, they nonetheless merit attention as an example of a single building managing to provide, within severe spatial constraints, contextual order, a convincing image, and appropriate living quarters for many families.

Dissolution

In 1928–1931 Walter S. Davis and his family lived in Italy. Upon his return to southern California, a disagreement be-

Left
El Greco, 1929, organizational
diagram.

Below left
El Greco, 1929, entrance
passageway into central courtyard.

Right
El Greco, 1929, front view with
landscaped and walled patios in
foregound.

Below right
El Greco, 1929, central courtyard
showing typical Andalusian
landscape.

tween the two brothers precipitated the dissolution of their partnership. Pierpont kept the office and all its documents, and Walter S. practiced out of his house, first in the French Village and then after 1940 in Palos Verdes. With the combined devastating effects of the depression and of the onslaught of Modern Architecture, the Davises practiced marginally after 1930. Walter S. had a notable involvement in a variety of Palos Verdes residential and commercial projects.

The Davises' Contribution

Even though the architectural oeuvre of the Davises covers scarcely ten years of intense effort, the effects of their practice were most important. Their 1915 publication of stock houses advocated in words and images a sensitive and balanced support of the Spanish house as a dominant housing vehicle for southern California, and their brand of studied eclecticism set a standard of the highest architectural quality.

The Gault Courts

The Los Angeles courts of Charles Gault appeared after the type had been firmly established by Zwebell and others. He can neither be called an innovator nor be said to have displayed the architectural connoisseurship of the Davis brothers, but Charles Gault's courtyard housing examples are distinguished works of architecture deserving of our attention.

Only three examples of his work have surfaced, all located in the Wilshire District and all built in the space of two short years. They are characterized by modest space standards for individual units, high densities, and generally large lots, which all occur on corners with accessibility.

Little is known of Gault himself, whose name does not appear in the professional literature of the period. It seems possible that he suddenly came upon the building type at the peak of its popularity and dropped it almost as quickly after popular demand and economic stability declined during the depression years. His efforts demonstrate rather poignantly how an almost anonymous builder working within the framework of the courtyard type could produce distinguished architecture. Certainly this ability to be so adopted is an indication of the universality of the type.

The Cochran Avenue Court
Wilshire District, 1928

The Cochran Avenue Court marks the purest attempt by Charles Gault to design courtyard housing in an uncompromisingly Andalusian mold. His two seminal contributions here are the accommodation of a regular parti on an irregular site and his insistence on formal definition based on irregular massing and profusion of detail.

The Cochran Avenue Court offers a series of important lessons on contextual responsibility. In the front of the building, the space between the orthogonally placed walls of the building and the angling street is made into private gardens defined by a brick wall. In the back, it is the mass of the building itself which is placed at an angle to the line of the alley. The outside surfaces are treated as public, ceremonious elements when they can be seen and read. They are transformed into Los Angeles stripped stucco facades when they

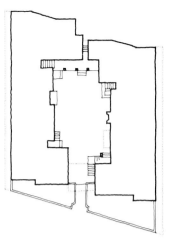

Above
Cochran Avenue Court, 1928,
organizational diagram.

Left
Cochran Avenue Court, 1928. A
courtyard landscaped in the typical
Los Angeles courtyard housing
manner.

119

are out of sight or lack importance. The building occupies and activates the whole site and offers messages to the public in appropriate places within its boundaries.

Entrance into the building is through a forecourt covered by the canopy of a large tree. The transition from street to courtyard is sensible and makes possible a gradual unfolding of the interior landscape. The scale of the courtyard is reduced by a deliberate shrinking of the scale of most architectural elements.

The dominant reading of the courtyard is based, not on its landscape, but rather on the irregular internal massing of the building. The ground plane is elaborately differentiated by tiled paths, parterres, and an ornate wellhead occupying its center. There is no strong canopy established by trees or other means, though, and most plants are actually pushed against the walls of the buildings without any elaborate spaces between them.

The combination of a dominant axial reading with strongly contrasting asymmetrical sides gives the courtyard of the Cochran Avenue Court a special sense of place. Its reduced scale and underplayed landscape create wonderful extensions for outdoor living for each of the individual dwellings.

Without doubt, there is a strong tendency in this court to pursue authentic Andalusian vernacular fragments. Charles Gault took pains to design and execute elements of genuine Hispanic flavor which animate this more than any other of his apartment buildings. Although the dwellings do not offer spectacular accommodations, they do nevertheless provide what may be regarded as the standard fare for the deluxe version of the courts.

The combination of site specificity and stylistic fidelity to the Andalusian prototypes makes the Cochran Avenue Court a substantial example of the courtyard housing typology.

Left
Cochran Avenue Court, 1928, aerial view.

Below left
Cochran Avenue Court, 1928, central courtyard featuring a well.

Opposite
Cochran Avenue Court, 1928, front view with landscaped and walled patios in the foreground.

Right
The Rosewood, 1929, detail of
staircase.

The Rosewood

Wilshire District, 1929

The Rosewood is one of the largest and most elegant of the courts of Los Angeles. It is a beautiful if slightly arcane building with a simple Italianate exterior and a complex courtyard derived from a variety of Mediterranean classical stylistic sources. Charles Gault, who the year before had built the Cochran Avenue Court in a pure vernacular Andalusian style, chose here to utilize more refined and consciously cultured references.

The Rosewood is located in a street dominated by dense duplex and apartment buildings. Its richly articulated portal overlayed on a plain and anonymous exterior is in keeping with the general nature of the surrounding buildings. The entrance, substantially set back from Sycamore Street, can best be interpreted as an accommodation of contextural conditions. A glimpse through the entranceway reveals a richly ornamented and landscaped courtyard. A variety of architectural elements, such as a large fireplace, arcaded porches, pilasters, and even freestanding columns of a bizarre, "homemade" composite order, dominate this courtyard. It is the overscaled fireplace and the low, ornate fountain and pool that first invite one to enter it.

The beautifully proportioned courtyard has the most complicated set of perimeter surfaces of all the Los Angeles deluxe courts. No two parts of it are similar. The northern end is filled with a freestanding staircase and a large olive tree. One of the two central sections is animated by a fishpond, the other by a two-story loggia on the east wall. The south end of the courtyard is raised over the rest of its surface and is articulated as a separate level out of which a special apartment gains access. Second-story dwellings are connected directly to the courtyard through stairs that are pulled into the body of the building and are represented as deep, dark recesses of space. The implied subdivision of the courtyard and its perimeter surfaces into smaller parts enhances the perception that the individual dwellings have special qualities, although the building is actually based on the idea of repeating, fairly typical one-bedroom apartments.

The accommodation of the automobile generates some of the genuinely special dwellings of the Rosewood. Most cars are stored in a carport on the east side of the building. A

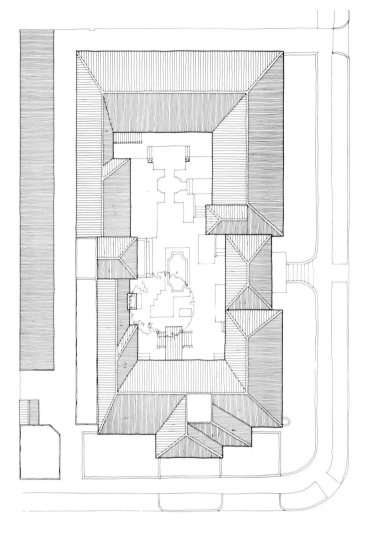

Above
The Rosewood, 1929, roof plan.

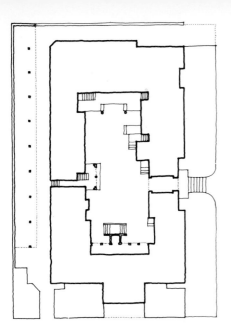

Above
The Rosewood, 1929, organizational diagram.

Below
The Rosewood, 1929, section.

Right
The Rosewood, 1929, Italianate arched entranceway into the central courtyard.

number of garages occur on the north side of the Rosewood, however, and these deserve special attention. They house cars on the street level, which is located half a level below the central courtyard. By raising the north-side apartments another half level, Gault made it possible for each of those apartments to open directly to a garden terrace above the garages, the terraces serving as lush private exteriors off the living areas of the dwellings.

Another unique dwelling opens to the raised terrace on the south side of the courtyard. A two-story living room constitutes its main design feature. Facing north, it receives sunlight through small, high windows on an upper mezzanine level. A staircase rises through the large space and leads to bedrooms on the mezzanine through a double-arched opening supported in the middle by a peculiar spiral column.

Although the richly varied courtyard and an occasional special feature can give the impression that the Rosewood was designed with luxury in mind, it is really very simply and economically planned and built. The only nonstandard apartment—the one described above—has a false fireplace. The other dwellings are not generous either in their quality or in their dimensions; few have balconies or other private extensions. Most of the parking is simple and sensible. The extravagant travertine entrance and various other decorative touches give the Rosewood the aura of an exclusive private world, but in fact it was probably developed on a modest budget and designed according to a highly pragmatic program. Its greatness consists in that it incorporates a simple conceptual base, is unusually picturesque, and has been uncompromisingly executed.

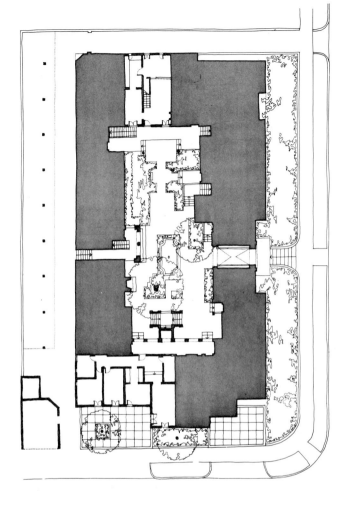

Above
The Rosewood, 1929, ground-floor plan.

Below left
The Rosewood, 1929, view from
passageway toward the fireplace
and porticoed stairway.

Below right
The Rosewood, 1929, central
courtyard with projecting staircase in
background.

Right
The Rosewood, 1929, private patios
over garage.

Below left
The Rosewood, 1929, living room
view of maisonette at southern edge
of courtyard. Note the sitting loft at
top of the stairs.

Below right
The Rosewood, 1929, living room
of maisonette at southern edge of
courtyard showing openings to
private patio.

The Sycamore

Wilshire District, 1930

The coming of the depression caused the collapse of the private-housing market but also precipitated an emotional shift away from the design of buildings that challenged the magical power of memory to transform reality and to render mere existence enjoyable.

The Sycamore, located directly across the street from the Rosewood, was perhaps the last of Charles Gault's great courts. It incorporates an array of all the important elements that characterize these wonderful buildings—the wooden balcony, the fountain, the great arched opening, the public fireplace, the grilled windows, the stepped-railing public staircase—but the intellectual crisis of the times is evident in their composition into a whole building.

The intended imagery of the Sycamore is surely Andalusian vernacular, but the execution displays a thinness of construction and a sparsity of detail that are indicative of what was to come in Los Angeles housing design. The overall square courtyard parti is established with strength, although the roof-line transitions on adjacent sides are less than certain. The four interior surfaces of the courtyard are designed as self-sufficient single facades that deliberately differ from each other.

The variety of the building surfaces in the courtyard contrasts quite sharply with the exterior imagery of the Sycamore. Wall elements are shallow and—at least in the front—symmetrically disposed, emphasizing the solidity of the building mass. That reading is further emphasized where a garden retaining wall lifts the ground off the sidewalk and establishes an idealized base for the court. Entrance is through a generous set of stairs and an arched passageway to the courtyard.

The dwellings are amenable but do not display special qualities. They are all connected directly to the garden by special stairs and passages instead of a public corridor. The garden is the center of attention from all parts of the building.

The courtyard landscapes of Charles Gault never quite reach the extraordinary quality of the gardens of the Zwebell and Davis courts. The Sycamore suffers from a fragmented landscape. The thinness of wooden members and the absence of articulated window frames or elaborate ironwork details make this building clearly representative of the last of the courtyard housing species.

Below
The Sycamore, 1930, view of the building from the entranceway of the Rosewood.

128

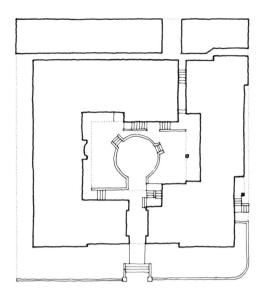

General Examples of Courts

The following eleven examples represent some of the most important courtyards in Los Angeles. No one protagonist stands out as the master designer of this group. Rather, they were executed by an assortment of architects and builders with varying skills, talents, and interests. They range in size from the diminutive Villa La Jolla to the village-scaled El Cadiz. Less than half were completed in the 1920s, with El Cadiz appearing very late, in 1936.

As a body of work, these buildings are truly remarkable, for despite their mixed pedigree they all contain extraordinary architectural qualities linking them to the courtyard type. All bear testimony to the potency of this living environment and its ability to be possessed by any and all who cared to take the time to understand its essentials.

Above left
The Sycamore, 1930, organizational diagram.

Left
The Sycamore, 1930, central courtyard with fountain and fireplace in the foreground.

129

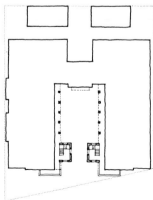

Above
Monterey Apartments, 1925,
entrance forecourt with symmetrical
palms, stairs, and openings.

Left
Monterey Apartments, 1925,
organizational diagram.

The Monterey Apartments

C. K. Smithley, Los Feliz, 1925

The Monterey is the oldest deluxe court in Los Angeles after the Villa Primavera. It was built in the Los Feliz district of the city at a time when there was doubt as to whether the exclusive suburbs of Hollywood would be developed toward the west or the east. Los Feliz ended up losing out to Beverly Hills, Brentwood, and Bel-Air, but some of its buildings are carried out with substantial force.

The Monterey, located on an irregular corner site, is designed so as to align with the side street. A triangular open space in the front becomes part of an elaborate entry sequence. The parti of the building is U shaped. The open part of the courtyard is spatially completed by the placement of two symmetrical stairways just off the major public side of the building. These stair towers define a forecourt on the sidewalk side which is embellished by two handsome *Washingtonia* palms. They also help enclose a courtyard that is thickly planted with succulents and cacti native to southern California.

The imagery pursued in this building is connected to a search for local as opposed to European architectural roots. As the name of the court suggests, it is designed with an eye toward expressions central to early California building. The simple stucco walls arranged in primary volumetric forms, the thin tile roofs, the simple, long wooden balconies, the naive arched openings are all common elements of the nineteenth-century adobe buildings of the area in and around Monterey. The use of California vernacular fragments in this court constitutes an unusually early eclectic experiment with the vernacular forms of central California.

The dense courtyard increases the isolation and privacy of individual dwellings. Some ground-floor units are unreasonably placed between a public path and a service alley. By and large, the dwellings are well finished, although they lack the dimension of exuberance which typically came about by identification with the movie industry or by attempts to connect with the comfortable memories of the past.

The Monterey can be seen as a valid attempt to energize regional building precedents as organizational and stylistic types. It opened the way for the creation of the accomplished courts of the late 1920s and still remains a vital place to live.

Above
Monterey Apartments, 1925, street view.

131

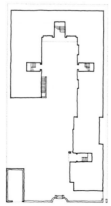

Above
Garfield Court, 1927, view of courtyard featuring large, arched living room openings on the ground level.

Left
Garfield Court, 1927, organizational diagram.

The Garfield Court

A. J. Waid, Hollywood, 1927

The source of the uniqueness of the Garfield Court is the location of its garage component and its relation to the formal development of the courtyard and the building.

A continuous wall along the sidewalk allows for two openings, each scaled to the size and ceremonial importance of the objects that enter through it. The pedestrian entrance is celebrated as a gate, and access to the courtyard is through a stair connecting up to the next half level. The garage entrance is offset to the south edge of the building; treated as an entranceway devoid of detail, it is reached through a ramp that leads down to the lower half level.

The garage is located underneath the foreshortened southern wing of the court. The space between the edge of this wing and the street is covered by a continuous surface of ivy. As one enters the courtyard, a set of trees provides a wide canopy that defines the forecourt as the transition between the building and the street. This forecourt becomes the completion of the courtyard on its open fourth side and highlights the difference between the two side wings.

The building's parti is a rare J shape in plan. The north wing extends almost all the way to the sidewalk and is three stories high. The south wing is shorter and is kept to two stories in height in order to let the sunlight reach the courtyard. The architecture is carried out in a strict Andalusian vernacular. The combination of style, massing, and landscape uniqueness render this piece of the building the visible expression of the garage that is housed underneath it.

The general impression is of a court made responsive to the realities of the context but not able to contribute to its visible definition in formal terms. It recedes quietly from the street, an introverted place. In typical fashion, its courtyard walls serve as the carriers of the stylistic realities of Mediterranean streets.

Above
Garfield Court, 1927, elaborate
entrance gate with courtyard
beyond.

133

Above
Garfield Court, 1927, detail of north
wall of courtyard.

The Villa de la Fuente

H. C. Nickerson, Jr., Wilshire District, 1928

The Villa de la Fuente is a most convincing application of the lessons inherent in Arthur Zwebell's design for the Andalusia. Three of the crucial formal and spatial aspects of the prototype were applied here by H. C. Nickerson, Jr.: the forecourt garage, entrance under a wooden balcony and a centrally located archway, and the definition of a regular central courtyard.

Seemingly a contradiction of good planning sense, parking forecourts can become elements of powerful architectural identity. In the Villa de la Fuente the garages are detached from the building and are treated as flanking service pavilions. The forecourt is articulated in space as a unique realm by being separated from the street by a walled gate. The covering of its ground surface in red paving tile gives it a special sense of urbanity and integrates it into the central courtyard. The forecourt is visually attached to the rest of the building and simultaneously detached from the realm of the blacktop-dominated street.

The main street facade of the building constitutes its most architecturally potent statement. An unusually wide, nine-bay wooden balcony and the typical ground-floor, iron-grilled Andalusian windows attach a special sense of dignity to the public rooms of the Villa de la Fuente. The central entranceway allows a glimpse of the interior patio but also subtly separates it from the forecourt.

The central courtyard is an unusual specimen among Los Angeles court central patios. It is square and regular both in plan and in elevation. It lacks the picturesqueness of the asymmetrical designs of Arthur Zwebell and his stress on authenticity of detail. Nonetheless, the simplicity and crispness of the elements generate a landscape of calmness and almost classical repose. The central fountain and the composition of arched windows behind it are the two dominant elements consciously styled for associational effect. The rest of the building is stated in Spanish Revival terms that are less than doctrinaire.

A noteworthy aspect of the central courtyard is that each unit has a walled private patio. These are similar to the ones present in the Villa d'Este in West Hollywood, also designed

Above
Villa de la Fuente, 1928, front facade
with parking forecourt.

Right
Villa de la Fuente, 1928,
organizational diagram.

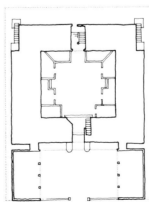

in 1928. The brick patio walls generate a second square layer of enclosure that defines space in the immediate surroundings of the fountain. Unusual Sevillian tile-surfaced benches are built into the patio walls. Trees and shrubs grow out of tightly defined planters in sharply limited parts of an otherwise exceptionally hard landscape. The succulents and cacti that inhabit the garden further reinforce the hardness of the courtyard.

Although lacking the lavish two-story living rooms of other courts, most dwellings are similarly entered through their enclosed private gardens. They are moderately designed by comparison to other deluxe courts. Stairs in the front and rear of the courtyard give access to several simple upper units. Still the typical pattern of large arched openings on the ground floor and balconied windows above dominates the cross axis of the building and also expresses the typical two-level arrangement of most of its dwellings.

The Villa de la Fuente is economically and sensibly carried out and incorporates a minimalist formal attitude that makes it particularly attractive and semantically accessible.

Above, opposite
Villa de la Fuente, 1928, central courtyard featuring walled private patios for each unit.

Above right
Villa de la Fuente, 1928, central courtyard with Andalusian fountain.

Below right
Villa de la Fuente, 1928, detail of tiled courtyard wall.

The Villa Madrid

Arthur W. Larson, West Hollywood, 1929

The Villa Madrid is a bold attempt to accommodate the court idea within an irregular context and to a program the complexity of which equals that of the Ronda. The site is doubly atypical in that it slopes sharply up from Miller Drive to the south and also is located on a corner. The combined effect of these two conditions is an oddly shaped ground plane. The court notion applied to this site was ingeniously distorted to maintain the type's generic organizational principles and yet to make it specific to the context.

The building parti is configured as an open U with one of the two legs distorted to pick up the roadway as it curves and climbs along the contours of the hill. Garages are located underneath the building and are accessible through an arched entranceway that is expressed at the scale of the building block of which it is a part. Entrance into the building is through a generous opening between the two legs of the U. These legs are serviced by a complex set of stairs and landscape elements (planters, hedges, and so on) that provide the transition from the street to the entry terrace.

The west side presents wide stretches of building to the view and gives the impression of overlapped housing blocks arranged parallel to the street. Indeed, the last block reaches Miller Drive as it turns the corner and becomes a strong street-defining element. On its sides and back, the building is beautifully manipulated to adjust to the edges of the site and made to respond to the formal clues of the irregular definitions of these edges by allowing space to be generated between itself and appropriate segments of the perimeter of the site.

Within the courtyard, all circulation is accommodated inside the body of the building. Public stairs are articulated as architectural elements integral to its overall form. The extreme elevational differences on the site are taken up by a terracing of the ground plane. The transition from the unfolding urban landscape of the interior of the courtyard to the opposing distant views of the city creates a sensational effect.

The Villa Madrid is one of the few courts carried out in a material other than the standard wood-and-stucco combination. The use of concrete brick is a reference to the work of

Arthur Zwebell as well as a quotation from early Los Angeles adobe buildings.

The degree of attention given to detail is unusually high. Window openings are very disciplined as a result of the use of masonry. Openings of many kinds are featured, there being a strong preference for arched windows in crucial, public parts of the courtyard. The woodwork is particularly unusual, with polychrome elements, including balconies, balustrades, staircases, windows, and doors, appearing in abundance.

The Villa Madrid contains many different kinds of dwellings. Although they are not spatially extravagant in the Zwebell tradition, they are nonetheless beautifully placed in unique positions within the whole building to take advantage of the specificity of the site. The views from many of the dwellings are exhilarating, and upper units have generous decks extending over the roofs of the lower units.

The degree of programmatic complexity and site specificity have turned the building into more than an object. It is convincingly carried out as an urban fragment, representative of a high degree of formal complexity. The sense of living in the Villa Madrid approaches that of the typical Mediterranean hill town. Walls define interior and exterior order whose validity is counted over time in terms of collective contribution and shared experience.

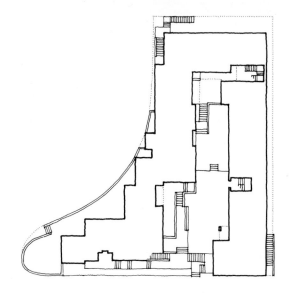

Above right
Villa Madrid, 1929, organizational diagram.

Below right
Villa Madrid, 1929, entrance into subterranean garage.

Left
Villa Madrid, 1929, front facade.

Below left
Villa Madrid, 1929, detail of stairway giving access to the upper units.

Below right
Villa Madrid, 1929, view of the elaborate central courtyard.

139

Above
Villa Madrid, 1929, detail of west wall
of courtyard.

The Cañon Court

J. Raymond, Beverly Hills, 1930

The Cañon Court was developed and built by C. R. Fargo, a contractor who was also responsible for the making of the Garfield Court. The two buildings are almost identical. For that reason, they are of special interest in the study of contextural effects on courtyard housing prototypes.

The massing of the Cañon Court is based on a complete, open U parti. The site is located at the intersection of a major boulevard with a typical small residential street. An alley runs parallel to the boulevard in the back part of the site.

Unlike its Hollywood counterpart, this building is based on the idea of the separation of pedestrian and car entrances. The garage is constructed in rough poured concrete and located half a level down from the alley. The pedestrian entrance is off Olympic Boulevard and is defined as an ornate iron gate. Access to the courtyard is half a level up from the sidewalk. This effective separation of cars from people creates all the advantages of being in a carefree place without sacrificing quick access to one's vehicle. Connection to the garage is provided through an ingenious combination of staircase and fountain, which together comprise the major object featured in the central courtyard.

Because the garage is located in the part of the site which borders on the alley, the section of the courtyard closest to the back block of the building is rendered as a hard, brick-covered patio. Four potted trees are placed in the center of this area. The courtyard segment nearest Olympic Boulevard is landscaped with a variety of trees, bushes, and natural groundcover. The entrance sequence from the sidewalk through a soft natural forecourt to a hard urban patio and finally to the building proper provides an intense set of experiences, rare for a site as small as this.

It is really remarkable that a building of the courtyard type stated in a Spanish Revival style can be transposed to a new site, maintaining its formal integrity and becoming contexturally responsive. It is even more surprising that the second version of a known building can appear as different from the source model as this one does simply by the application of a basic set of formal moves that make it site specific.

Above
Cañon Court, 1930, street view.

Right
Cañon Court, 1930, organizational
diagram.

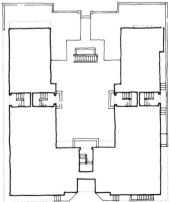

141

Left
Cañon Court, 1930, plain walls on secondary street and alley sides.

Below left
Cañon Court, 1930, central court as seen through gateway.

El Pasadero

Jason and Irene Reese, West Hollywood, 1931

El Pasadero is a rare example of a court in which the complex narrative of the exterior of the building is stressed at the expense of the quality of its interior courtyard. In a conscious reversal of court practices, the exterior street space is designed as a series of soft surfaces and objects.

The drama of entering is played out in a series of contradictory readings generated along the entry path. Perhaps the strongest ambiguous message occurs at street level, where the automobile entrance is expressed as the dominant opening into the building, overshadowing a pair of symmetrical stepped-railing staircases.

Two front towers are nearly equal in height, width, and massing, but they are rendered different by a variation in their plan shape, their unequal volumetric development, and the dissimilar shapes of their roofs, wall openings, and surface appliqués. These towers are connected in order to complete the enclosure of the courtyard. Two separate devices are used to carry out this formal connection: the false screen in the front and the two-story loggia at the back of the entry forecourt. Although the screen is more visible and evident as the demarcation of pedestrian entry, it is actually the loggia that marks the transition into the interior of the building. Living-unit design within El Pasadero provides examples of deluxe accommodation. Next to modest living quarters, the front and middle sections of the court contain maisonette units with wonderful volumetric qualities. Sandwiched in between are the simpler one-story units.

The details of the building are crisp. There is a mixture of vernacular and erudite stylistic quotations throughout, and both these types of Spanish Revival fragments are executed convincingly. An ornate Palladian window dominates the north side of the courtyard and, with equal force, the simple Andalusian arches describe the loggia. Ironwork, woodwork, and tile work of quality make the intended mixed imagery of the building possible.

The physical dimensions of the courtyard and the multiplicity of details on its surrounding walls make El Pasadero resemble the Arab callejons of southern Spain. The intentional contradictions and variety of stylistic means generate powerful readings that recall urban memories and suggest a possible Los Angeles that never came to be.

Below
El Pasadero, 1931, street facade featuring asymmetrical towers and separated entrances for cars and pedestrians.

Right
El Pasadero, 1931, organizational diagram.

Below left
El Pasadero, 1931. Elaborate stairs lead to the upper level and entrance into the courtyard.

Below right
El Pasadero, 1931, view of courtyard through loggia.

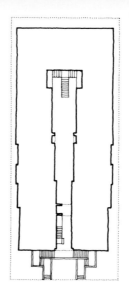

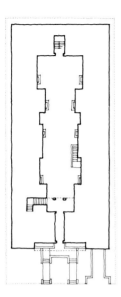

The Villa Sevilla

Elwood Houseman, West Hollywood, 1931

The Villa Sevilla is a typical example of a postdepression court. It was built according to the most refined principles of courtyard housing design but lacks the strength of detail which characterized earlier experiments with an Andalusian vernacular vocabulary.

The garage for the building is located underground, and the entrance into the courtyard is separated by a substantial difference of elevation from the street. The expression afforded the building on its Harper Avenue front is descriptive of the single house; the balcony and small windows represent a residential scale that is not related to communal living.

The courtyard is surprisingly large and uniform. Its uniformity is in part due to the lack of strong appliqué detail and the fact that standard metal-sash windows were used throughout. The surprisingly large scale is generated by the regularity of the space, a continuously paved ground plane, the four marvelous coconut palms planted in the center, and the strong reading of the edges of the courtyard as an unbroken container.

The most elaborate formal feature of the building is the treatment of these walls. The entrance sequence allows one passage through an arcaded portico before entering the courtyard proper. The termination of the entrance axis is expressed as an elaborate three-story wall replete with various balconied extensions. The public formality of the two short courtyard-enclosing walls is contrasted by the relative blandness of the two long walls. Most dwellings are directly entered through these long surfaces, and most living rooms are also located behind them with direct visual access to the courtyard. Still, the architecturally most dominant elevations remain the ones connected to the axis of entry.

The individual dwellings allow for considerable amenity, although they are of limited architectural value. The building as a whole is a strong application of the deluxe court formula to a typical Los Angeles urban site. Despite weak building details and a routine garden, the Villa Sevilla remains a substantial contribution to a special Los Angeles way of building and living.

Above left
Villa Sevilla, 1931, roofscape.

Above right
Villa Sevilla, 1931, street facade with
elaborate Monterey-style balcony.

Left
Villa Sevilla, 1931, view of powerful
formal courtyard from entranceway.

The Barcelona and the Coruña Apartments

George Fosayke, Los Feliz, 1932

While the Barcelona and the Coruña are examples of the simplest, most elementary type of courtyard building, together they demonstrate how freestanding buildings, each complete and independent, can complement one another spatially and formally to create coherent groups of structures with unitary characteristics and great urban presence.

The Barcelona and the Coruña are symmetrically disposed buildings of L-shaped massing. They shape an elaborate street parterre and entranceway and help define an interior garden space from which all apartments gain access. This upper garden, separated from the sidewalk, is sparsely landscaped and not fully enclosed, as it would be in one of the more visually elaborate courts.

The two buildings share important qualities that encourage one to read them as an ensemble. They are both set back and raised from the street, and their street-front landscapes are designed on common principles. The Los Feliz Boulevard elevations of both buildings extend almost to the property line at each side. The length and continuity of this "wall" is further heightened because the arched driveway to the rear garages in each building penetrates the street surface but does not seriously erode it. The second-floor balcony of the Coruña extends two bays along the front of the Barcelona, establishing a clear sense of horizontal continuity. Identical heights, similarities in the wall openings, and balcony and roof details reinforce the impression of one building: it becomes a somber public, urban facade to the street, creating a private, if slightly undernourished, garden world in its interior.

The lesson is obvious: Buildings have to be neither attached nor identical to create a sense of urban continuity and presence. Simple spatial ideas and architectural details skillfully applied can establish a widely shared formal vocabulary that is impossible in sets of buildings that are perceptually or conceptually disconnected.

It is remarkable that the translator of these simple ideas into form was not an architect but an engineer, George Fosdyke. It is ample proof that the lesson of this court is not only obvious but also simple and modestly applicable toward the creation of both meaningful single buildings.

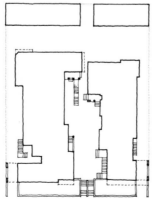

Above
The Barcelona and the Coruña,
1932, street view.

Left
The Barcelona and the Coruña,
1932, organizational diagram.

Above
The Barcelona and the Coruña,
1932, detail of entrance stairway and
elaborate balconies on front
facades.

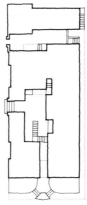

Above
Villa La Jolla, 1933, small-scale
pavilions fronting side street.

Left
Villa La Jolla, 1933, organizational
diagram.

The Villa La Jolla

George Fosdyke, Los Angeles, 1933

The Villa La Jolla is a court of diminutive scale. It is a straight example of the closed-courtyard parti type, but the development of its massing is unique. The building occupies a corner site. The parts of it that border on the two streets are expressed as a series of connected one-story blocks. The remaining two sides of the building are designed as a continuous two-story block. The massing idea becomes visible as a set of two intersecting L-shaped blocks, different in massing and defining a central courtyard.

The relatively low profile on the street sides of the Villa La Jolla disguises the intensity of the residential use of the site. At first sight, the building appears to be a simple dwelling. What is gained from this is a degree of site specificity that allows the definition of an ample public front yard along Olympic Boulevard, a tight urban sidewalk on La Jolla Avenue, and a wonderul garden patio between the back of the building and the freestanding garage block.

The central courtyard is almost devoid of attention to landscape and because of its small size serves exclusively as a passage of no architectural importance. By contrast, the details of the building itself are mixed. The low exterior block is carried out as a rigorous example of Andalusian vernacular revival. A few details stand out particularly: the wood-and-stucco bay window, the tiled, pyramidal fireplace chimney, and the dovecotes on the sides of the entry to the courtyard. The high interior block is less consistent in the purity of its detail but remains a fair attempt at quality Spanish Revival construction.

Above
Villa La Jolla, 1933, detail of entry into private patio.

151

El Cadiz

Milton J. Black, Hollywood, 1936

El Cadiz was the last major Spanish Revival court constructed in Los Angeles. Both its strengths and its weaknesses as an idea and as a building arise out of this fact. Its designer, Milton J. Black, was an accomplished Moderne stylist who obviously could change design idioms to fit building types or client idiosyncracies.

According to the present owners, El Cadiz was inspired by earlier Zwebell buildings in West Hollywood. Any specific formal reference to particular courts, however, is difficult to trace. There is nonetheless a vague ambience, generated both by building details and by outdoor spaces, which is reminiscent not only of the original Andalusian prototypes but also of their Zwebellian transformations.

A glance at the plan reveals the simplicity and genius of the conceptual basis of this building. The typical regular courtyard with a small central garden has been greatly enlarged. In order that a misproportioned leftover void not be created in this process of enlarging, though, smaller peninsulas of building have been attached to the inside of the perimeter wall. These village-scale penetrations reduce the overall size of the interior voids and generate smaller courtyards to which clusters of dwellings are attached. Each peninsula is a unique two-story building with its own stairs, porches, balconies, and other special architectural features. The overall impression is not one of a single building but one of substantial urban fragments making for a lively street and plaza scene.

Although El Cadiz contains a great variety of interesting dwellings, they do not have the spatial excellence of the Zwebellian prototypes. Still, the concept of articulating each part of the building as a separate set of dwellings with its own stairs and special features while maintaining an overall unitary reading is carried out convincingly. The curse of anonymous "apartments" has seldom been more skillfully disguised.

The typical Spanish fragments—tiled roofs, paved courtyards, porches, balconies, arched windows, and ornate doors—are all present. These elements are the first-generation descendants of the original Andalusian pro-

Above
El Cadiz, 1936, central courtyard
defined by a variety of building
elements.

Right
El Cadiz, 1936, organizational
diagram.

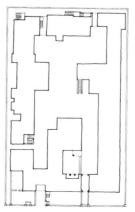

totypes. But the ingenious underground parking garage, the compositional overlap of village-scale fragments, and the discipline of a multicourtyard plan are all extensions of ideas developed by Zwebell, primarily in the Ronda, and they make it possible for us to classify El Cadiz as a second-generation Spanish Revival building.

The fundamental weakness of this building lies in the fact that it was constructed under the conditions of a depression economy. Despite formal similarities to the courts of the 1920s, its space standards, construction, and execution are visibly thinner than those of the earlier courts. The appeal of authenticity based on precise copying and execution of Mediterranean original fragments is here lost in the attempt to economize through the use of standard elements and the cutting out of highly crafted details.

The simple facade of El Cadiz generates a public and urban presence on the street and hides an intimate and complex world of evocative places and objects inside. One is bound to feel respectful here, experiencing the last of a lost species: the deluxe Spanish Revival apartment court.

Top
El Cadiz, 1936, articulated dwelling on north side of courtyard.

Bottom
El Cadiz, 1936, front facade.

Top
El Cadiz, 1936, general view of
interlocking open spaces.

Bottom
El Cadiz, 1936, front facade detail
showing garage entrance.

Echo Park Terraced Courts

Although strictly speaking Echo Park is as much a part of Los Angeles as, for instance, Hollywood, its special conditions have generated some unique housing forms. The courts of Echo Park are no exception to this rule and therefore deserve special mention.

The pronounced rolling hills of the Echo Park district were stubbornly subjected to the grid. The resulting imposition of regular building lines over irregular terrain tended to encourage orthogonal building development, albeit at times with daring sectional treatment born out of necessity.

In addition to these physical factors, development tended to be dense because of the close proximity of the district to downtown Los Angeles. Accommodations are uniformly modest, as the pressure to pack many units on limited land was particularly acute.

The two examples shown here demonstrate and express these special Echo Park characteristics. What is amazing is that even within the constraints of sloping sites, tight budgets, and extremely high density, the court parti was ingeniously and successfully adapted. No better argument could be made for the universality of the court type than to see its transformation within the very specific context of Echo Park.

The Vendome Avenue Courts

Grace Roe and J. D. Gilbert, Echo Park, 1929–1931

The twin buildings of the Vendome Avenue Courts are unparalleled among courts in their ability to shape the form of the city. It is obvious that in precise typological terms the two are not comparable to the normative housing examples based on the idea of a closed courtyard; but their unique city-defining qualities do merit attention and study.

The parti of the Vendome Courts is defined by housing blocks that occupy the back part of the site and are parallel to the street and by longer housing slabs connecting the back blocks to the street. The building's figure-field reading emphasizes the front slabs as dominant, massive elements separated by thin layers of space. These spaces resemble more a village street than a courtyard. They are alternatively defined as public and service paths. The public passages are carefully terraced, and their landscaping accentuates the attributes of the individual terraces.

Cars are accommodated at the sidewalk level. In one of the two courts, a broken pediment motif overlaid on the front elevation provides a strong architectural representation of the garage at the scale of the whole building. The asymmetrical design of the mass and surface of the lower housing blocks renders the symmetry of the garages even more powerful. The first level of building off the sidewalk is expressed as a regular continuous base on top of which there opens an irregular form.

The most important formal discovery incorporated in the second court is the unfolding of symmetrical exterior public staircases that are tucked into the outer skin of the building. Every major landing off the staircase network becomes an entrance platform into a dwelling. The discipline of this architectural idea is softened only by stereotypical Spanish Revival stylistic gestures.

The roofs of the two courts are conceived with little connection to the architectural nature of the housing blocks. Their styling is applied onto the blocks as masses in space. Tiled mansard roofs and mixed flat and sloping roofs, when combined with geometrically impure surface patterns, generate a sense of general iconographic confusion. One identifies such diversity with urban precincts rather than mere single buildings.

Above
Vendome Courts, 1929-1931, front
facade of building to the north.

Right
Vendome Courts, 1929-1931,
organizational diagrams.

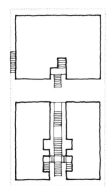

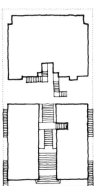

The sloping of the site allows the back block to be placed in a position of compositional and visual dominance. The lower blocks are also arranged to respond to the slope of the hill. The formal moves that render the building site responsive result in an overall massing for both buildings which is very fragmented. In this way, individual units gain access to the view and the sun, and the buildings as a whole assume their intended imagery as a part of a Mediterranean hill town.

Space accommodation in both Vendome Avenue Courts is minimal, and the two buildings have for a long time accommodated inhabitants of modest incomes. The incorporation of important architectural principles in such minor buildings runs counter to established common wisdom. The fact that the principles are transformed into a visible urban and architectural order elevates the two Vendome Courts to the level of significant examples for future design action.

Above right
Vendome Courts, 1929-1931, general view of the courts in their Echo Park hillside context.

Below right
Vendome Courts, 1929-1931, street view showing terraced profile of both buildings.

The Big Mama Court

Nathan Black, Echo Park, 1932

The Big Mama Court was recently christened by the authors in honor of its tenacious manager. As a building it is only peripherally related to the closed-courtyard parti buildings examined in these case studies. Both the location and the quality of the construction suggest that it was not meant to be inhabited by the glamorous citizens of Los Angeles. It was intended as a typical apartment house, and it has followed the fate of Echo Park as a whole by accommodating an increasingly low income population.

The organization of the Big Mama Court is based on the idea of arranging eight housing blocks on one site in such a way that they define positive and meaningful space between them. The housing blocks are similar in massing and detailed expression, but the court as a whole is site specific to the extent that the blocks get transformed by reference to context.

The Echo Park Avenue side of the building reads both as an entrance and at a scale larger than the single housing block. This occurs because the two front blocks are connected by a parabolic archway. Entrance is into a stepped-up, narrow, and exceptionally hard courtyard. No doorways or other major architectural elements belonging to individual dwellings open onto this courtyard. Despite the existence of a small fountain, this unusual courtyard is carried out like a public narrow street of dimensions and light quality that are intensely Mediterranean.

The courtyard is intersected at ninety degrees by minor passages that lead to garages on the side street. These garages are integrated into the mass of the building, creating a recession from the outside surface. Their repetition along the whole side of the building creates a wonderful pattern and an appropriate public, car-related face onto the street.

The individual apartments are small and not particularly amenable. The cut-rate, depression Spanish Revival styling is reminiscent of the thin, cut-rate boom Spanish Revival styling of the 1960s. The essential quality of the Big Mama Court lies in the application of a clear organizing idea to a strong context. The idea is transformed into a building that is expressive in architectural terms of both organizational principles and the genius loci of the site.

Above
Big Mama Court, 1932, front facade.

159

Above
Big Mama Court, 1932, detail of
arched openings into garages and
stairways.

Right
Big Mama Court, 1932,
organizational diagram.

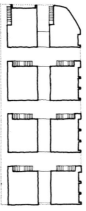

Above left
Big Mama Court, 1932, rear facade
and view into elongated central
courtyard.

Above right
Big Mama Court, 1932, general view
of side facade.

Right
Big Mama Court, 1932, detail of
stairway leading to upper units.

161

Pasadena Courts

At the turn of the century, the city of Pasadena rapidly developed into a winter resort for wealthy vacationers from the East. This surge of newcomers prompted a demand for lavish hotels as well as modest temporary accommodations. The latter found expression in the charming bungalow courts that dot Pasadena to this day.

These rental units characteristically occurred on a single lot surrounding a common space or road, making a kind of miniature street scene. Later, in the 1920s, permanent accommodations became necessary for the increasing numbers who settled here. The bungalow court idea solidified into a denser continuous wall of units surrounding an urban patio or courtyard. The Greene and Greene stick style was replaced by the white of the Spanish Revival, resulting in several excellent examples of courtyard housing just outside of Los Angeles.

La Casa Torre

Edward P. Babcock, Architect; Frederick H. Ruppel, Builder;
Pasadena, 1924

The following is reprinted from a real estate promotional brochure of the period:

One of the fine Mediterranean structures on the Riviera of Southern California is La Casa Torre . . . eight distinctive homes, laid end-to-end, grouped under one roof around an exceptionally large patio.

A home of unusual grace and beauty awaits you here.

An exterior view of La Casa Torre reveals the stateliness and dignity suggestive of a private home of splendid proportions. Every tradition of the finest Mediterranean architecture has been employed to avoid the bleak outlook of monotony (characteristic of many apartments) without destroying the architectural unity of the building.

The spacious patio's surface is paved with Padre antique block tile, rich red in color, broken by large mazes of shrubbery on either side of a central fountain. A profusion of potted plants, both large and small, is placed around the patio as well as on the various balconies and stairways. These combine with multi-colored tile window boxes to heighten the impression of Continental atmosphere.

Exceptional care has been taken in the choice of Spanish, Italian and Moorish arches to blend each into the general scheme of architecture. The many interesting lines of grills, arches and balconies intrigue the imagination and complete the picture of Old World Romance.

Each one of these homes is as distinctive and unusual as the home you would select if purchasing. Each has features to appeal to the needs and tastes of the individual family. Some have all the rooms on one floor, while in others the master bedrooms are above. Some ceilings conform to the lines of the building; some are arched; while still others are beamed with the massive beams of the Trentini or the more delicate beams of Cordova and Seville. The plain masonry of one exterior balcony gives place to the delicate iron tracery of a later period in another.

An outstanding feature, common to each apartment, is the large size living room. The smallest of these is approximately sixteen feet by twenty-one feet. Each, though distinctive in appointment and design, is modeled along the same lines of spaciousness and dignity. All have natural wood fireplaces of unglazed tile, which is also used in the entryways.

Every effort has been employed to create an air of dignified luxury. The wrought iron curtain rods and grills, the balustrades and the lighting brackets and lamps of correct period and design will combine unobtrusively with the furnishings and draperies of your selection.

The bedrooms have their own private tiled bath and ample clothes presses or clothes closets or both. Throughout each apartment there is an abundance of closets, cupboard room and storage space.

All the glamor and charm of Moorish castles, Italian villas and Spanish haciendas are here combined with the superlative in electrical convenience and comfort.

Each apartment is completely isolated, both as to walls and ceilings, by the best sound insulation materials known to modern building. The effectiveness of this insulation is said to be treble that used in the average structure of this kind.

Six or seven rooms . . . furnished, if you like.

Above
Casa Torre, 1924, partial street
facade.

Right
Casa Torre, 1924, organizational
diagram.

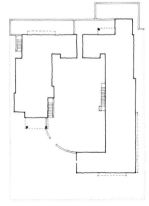

Above
Casa Torre, 1924, detail of courtyard
featuring a secondary loggia above
a dwelling entrance.

Opposite
Casa Torre, Pasadena, 1924. An
original promotional image by its
architect, Edward P. Babcock.

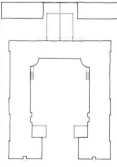

Above
West California Court, 1927, street view through palms.

Left
West California Court, 1927, organizational diagram.

West California Street Residence Apartments

Robert Ainsworth, Pasadena, 1927

The following is reprinted from the *Pasadena Star-News,* June 9, 1928:

Establishment of a handsome, substantial and pictorial assemblage of apartment houses, collected under one roof and forming a striking addition to the residential development of the locality, has been completed at 339–351 West California Street. Designed by Robert H. Ainsworth, a Pasadena architect whose work is rapidly gaining him repute, the structure contains eight homes, artistically assembled about a picturesque court and attractively situated in one of the most pleasing residential areas in the southwest section of the community.

There is a genuine spirit of artistic beauty about the aggregation of apartment houses which Mr. Ainsworth has developed. Following the Spanish-Mediterranean style of architecture, that is playing so significant a part in the upbuilding of the Southland, the property is certainly one of the choicest additions that has yet been made to the residential development of the community. Expressions of an artistic character have been brought to the courtyard, the fountain, the corners and the roof lines of the structure, the entire group making an imposing and impressive ensemble of very fine interest and charm.

While one roof covers the entire group of houses, the apartments have the characteristics of private homes. Each home has its own number, its own public service conveniences, such as telephone, electric light and gas equipment and other features, not customary in apartment houses. Then, the apartments are of two stories, again arranged in the manner of the average sized residence with living rooms and dining rooms on the lower floors, the bedrooms and concomitant features on the upper floors.

An exterior glimpse of the apartments shows a fine structure, admirable in architectural lines, choice in building and artistic finish. All the homes center about the fountain, in the landscaped court. The property runs to a depth of 250 feet, offering ideal opportunities for the fine landscaping policies which have been developed. The frontage is 154 feet. The courtyard has all the spaciousness of a large sized lot.

There is nothing uniform about the appearance of the apartments. Interesting architectural features make each residence distinctive. Here a doorway is sunk into a broad wall; there the doorway is centered in a tower-like corner. Windows are made pictorial with grills; tiles adorn the stairways, lend color to the fountain. The garden and patios are typical of the Andalusian gardens of Spain, laid out with the thought of maintaining privacy for the individual homes.

Internally, the homes are equally successful. The general scheme has been to erect a seven-room house. Each has three master bedrooms, and two baths, on the upper floors; a maid's room and bath

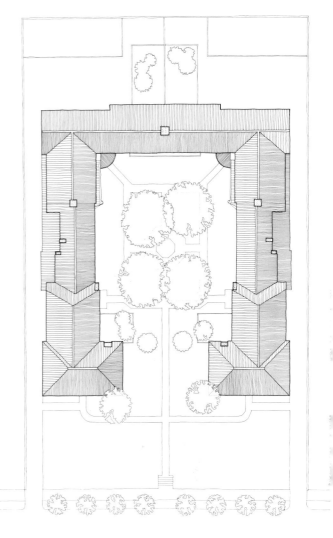

Above
West California Court, 1927, roof plan.

Above
West California Court, 1927,
ground-floor plan.

are on the lower floors. Bedrooms are 14 by 16 feet. Living rooms are 16 by 24 feet and dining rooms are 14 by 16 feet. It will be realized that they are spacious. Four of the apartments have sleeping porches; all have basements, generous in their storage space. Two apartments in the rear have private patios, further enhancing the pleasing outdoor features which mark the court as a whole. Garages for twelve cars bring up the rear of the property, obscured, yet easily approached by paved driveways on either side of the project.

Of frame and plaster construction, the buildings are particularly substantial. Insulation has been provided between all rooms and apartments and the plumbing fixtures are soundless, the latest insulating methods being employed. Hand made lamps and other fixtures adorn both interior and exterior walls; tiles are used with fine effect in many places.

Interior decoration of the homes has been a feature. Downstairs, walnut effects have been secured; upstairs, old ivory tones are pleasing and plaster walls of parchment color are distinctive. Fireplaces are in all the main rooms and many of the master bedrooms.

In designing the structure, Mr. Ainsworth has aimed at artistic effect and utilitarian values. He has achieved both. The entire ensemble of the homes is one of peculiar beauty; the individuality of each residence has nevertheless been retained. A heavy tile roof; artistically placed doors and windows; the cool beauties of the patio with its fountain; the broad garden effects of the courtyard and other interesting and artistic features readily capture the imagination. The complete and finished quality of the work is very noticeable and the varied and important conveniences in the interior layout of the homes are of pronounced worth.

The property is situated in close proximity to South Orange Grove Avenue, in one of the most delightful residential localities of the Southwest. The group of homes makes a very distinctive addition to the fine residential qualities of the neighborhood and the homes should appeal to those clients who prefer to have the advantages of the private home maintained, in an ideal place, where the advantageous features of combined facilities are available.

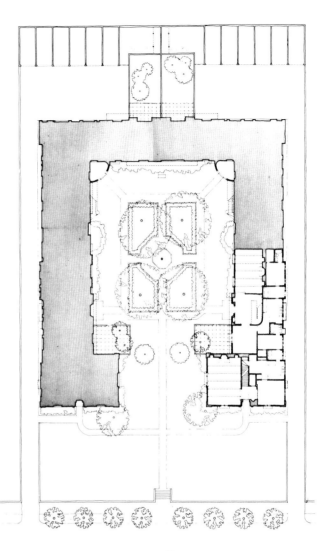

Above
West California Court, 1927, central courtyard with fountain.

Above left
West California Court, 1927, detail of
northwest corner of courtyard with
circular entrance portico.

Left
West California Court, 1927,
streetscape along service drive.

Above left
West California Court, 1927, detail of
northwest corner of courtyard with
stairway to upper level.

Above right
West California Court, 1927,
roofscape along service drive.

Right
West California Court, 1927, parking
garages in rear.

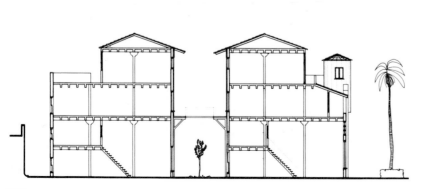

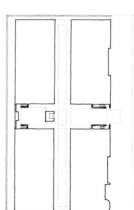

Mixed-Use Courts

The courtyards studied up to this point have been exclusively residential. Obviously, however, the typological notion of courtyard is not limited to housing alone. To demonstrate this point we have included two extraordinary mixed-use courts. They adhere to the canon established by the courtyard housing examples in that they simultaneously enclose private courts and define the public street. They make good urban neighbors and suggest a vision for the city which is as provocative as it is practical.

The Granada Buildings
Franklin Harper, Los Angeles, 1925

The Granada Buildings are located directly across from the lovely extension of LaFayette Park and less than one block from bustling Wilshire Boulevard. The four buildings that constitute the ensemble are arranged along a north-south axis in such a way as to create three layers of open space: the street, the central court, and the service court. These three places are differentiated by dimension, landscape, and the quality of the building surfaces that surround them. Exterior space is consciously treated as a positive element and becomes the dominant organizing idea for the entire building. The central entry and central space create shaded areas that serve both as places and as movement channels. All the public spaces in the building open directly into these "outdoor rooms." The central court, therefore, begins to accept all the attributes of the traditional narrow commercial street.

The four blocks, despite the seeming complexity and picturesque treatment of the exterior surfaces, are in reality highly repetitive and rational as a plan and sectional idea. Each block is composed of six slots in plan, corresponding to the structural module. The slots are arranged four layers deep in section, defining two maisonettes stacked one on top of the other. The upper units are accessible from an upper gallery, which occurs at the third level. Each maisonette is made up of one large two-story space with a small mezzanine opposite the entry side. The large spaces on the ground were intended as stores, with their mezzanines designed as storekeepers' efficiency apartments, and the upper maisonettes were intended as apartments or artists'/artisans'

Above
Cortijo near Ronda in southern Spain. The massing of the Granada Buildings suggests an almost literal copying of this fine old building.

Above, opposite
Granada Buildings, 1925, street view from extension of LaFayette Park.

Below left, opposite
Granada Buildings, 1925, section.

Below right, opposite
Granada Buildings, 1925, organizational diagram.

173

studios. The extreme mix of uses and people in the original concept of the building created the precondition for a vital and diverse way of life, one quite unique in this region. The imagery of the building as an urban fragment with streets is expressive of the way of life it was intended to generate.

The structure consists of a regular grid of wooden columns that have been enclosed on the periphery by a brick load-bearing wall. This organization permits extraordinary spatial adaptability over time. Within this framework one can subdivide in almost free-plan fashion a variety of combinations of rental space. Today many of the original slots have been harmoniously fused with neighboring units into larger, commodious rental spaces.

The exterior surfaces of the Granada Buildings reinforce the idea of city fragment. The central court openings are highly differentiated in terms of the various "row house" slots that constitute it. Each slot is allowed its own expression; the two-dimensional organization of doors and windows in every slot generates an overall surface pattern that stresses variety and individual choice. The pattern becomes suggestive of the city fabric, where one deals not with one building, but with many attached ones.

The front of the building facing LaFayette Park is equally explicit about the nature of its organization. The ground floor accepts and underscores the nature of the street in terms of massing and setbacks. All the commercial establishments in the front two Granadas open directly onto the sidewalk. The building surfaces at the front display a remarkable reversal from the surfaces of the central court. The single attached expression has been suppressed in favor of a reading of coupled slots. Moreover, the basic idea of the section of the building as a sandwich of two maisonettes has also been suppressed in favor of a reading of sometimes three or four undifferentiated stories.

The front surface is given a life of its own. One can see it as a discreet design problem controlled by four interrelated scales. The first scale aims to relate the building to the size of the city as a whole. The second scale attempts to explain the nature of the structure of the building as a discreet object. The third scale is expressive of the nature of each room within the building. The fourth scale concentrates on the expression of the individuality of particular elements at the level of component (doors, windows, etc.). These four scales are so balanced that they reinforce each other to the point that they cannot be separated.

Finally, the side elevations of the Granadas are bold outlines of their space structure in section. They suggest the possibility of continuation of the building idea to encompass many more Granadas in the future.

The Granada Buildings have attained an almost mythic quality in the Los Angeles design world, as architects, graphic designers, and artists have made it their home. The court is one of the monuments of southern California architecture and one that contains the seeds of an urban existence whose promise was never fulfilled. This example beautifully demonstrates how the courtyard housing type can be adapted to respond to high-density and mixed-use demands.

Above right
Granada Buildings, 1925, roof plan.

Right
Granada Buildings, 1925, front elevation.

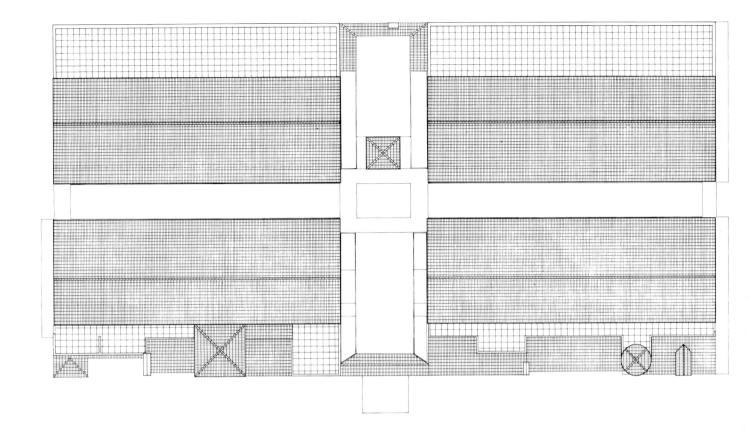

175

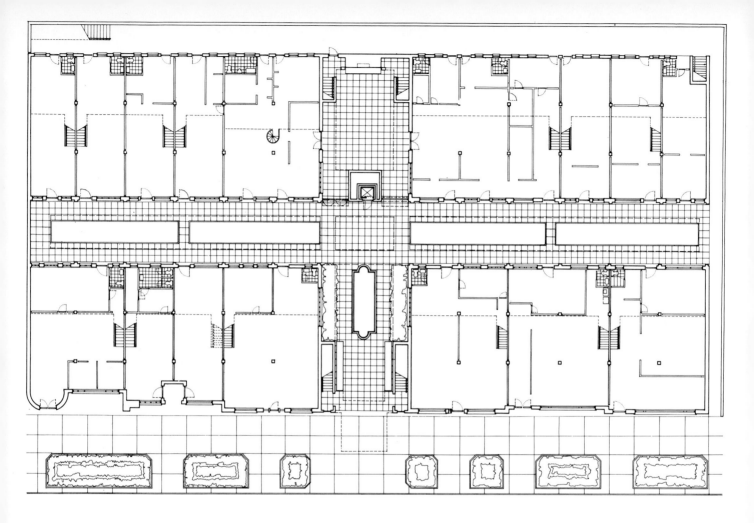

Above, opposite
Granada Buildings, 1925,
ground-floor plan.

Below, opposite
Granada Buildings, 1925, courtyard elevation, west.

Above left
Granada Buildings, 1925, central
courtyard with gallery access above.

Above right
Granada Buildings, 1925, rear wall
with services superimposed on it.

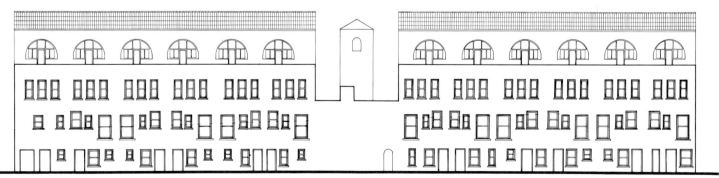

Above, opposite
Granada Buildings, 1925, multiple
module office maisonette.

Below, opposite
Granada Buildings, 1925, rear
elevation.

Above left
Granada Buildings, 1925, oblique
view showing deeply layered front
facade.

Above right
Granada Buildings, 1925, typical
interior office maisonette.

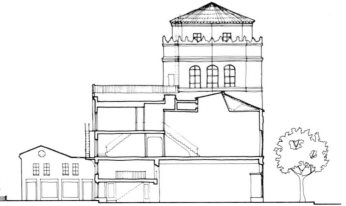

Above
Chapman Park Studios, 1928, street view with articulated corner towers framing entry into Alexandria Avenue.

Left
Chapman Park Studios, 1928, section.

The Chapman Park Studios

Morgan, Walls, and Clements, Los Angeles, 1928

Stiles Clements emerged as one of the finest Los Angeles architectural stylists in a career that spanned almost fifty years, from the 1910s to 1965. His contribution was unique in that in the early part of his life he produced a great number of the eclectic monuments for this city, including the Atlantic Richfield Building, the Mayan Theater, and the Samson Rubber and Tire Company, while in his later years, after a change of heart and an adoption of Modern Architecture, he was responsible for some of the great buildings of the forties and fifties, including a number of Wilshire Boulevard corporate commissions: the Broadway department store, the Carnation Company headquarters, and the Transport Indemnity Building.

One of the little-known contributions of the Clements firm has been the design in the twenties and thirties of a great number of mixed-use corner buildings in a Spanish Revival style. These buildings are a familiar part of the Los Angeles urban landscape. The Chapman Park Studios were part of that combined courtyard and corner building typology.

The sectional development of the building is remarkable. Its base is made up of a row of stores, two storied on the street with a mezzanine level in the rear. The top two floors contain two-level maisonette studio/apartments. An interior corridor at the second floor gives access to these unusual dwellings, which are arranged with a large, two-story-high, skylighted studio/living space facing the street on one side and a kitchen and small dining space overlooking a rear courtyard on the other. Interior stairs connect each side to a bedroom and bath. The idea of the long through apartment with spaces interlocking about a corridor occurring at alternate levels is a precursor to the famous *rue intérieure* of the Unité at Marseilles.

Actually, Le Corbusier might have benefited from a knowledge of Chapman Park. The Unité corridor was an interior space without natural light, but in Chapman Park natural light penetrates the corridor because the wall that separates it from the living rooms is defined by floor-to-ceiling translucent glass windows. Entrance into these rooms is through large glass doors. By contrast, all the small rooms of the dwellings, both private and public, are collected in the

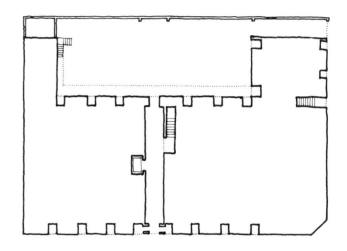

Above
Chapman Park Studios, 1928,
organizational diagram.

courtyard side of the building. The entrance wall defining this side is opaque, and the doors are also solid, reinforcing the impression of privacy and difficulty of access. A set of stairs connects the rooms within the courtyard side of the studios, and a second one descends from the top bedrooms, over the rue intérieure, and down into the living rooms. The ingenious spatial arrangement provides splendid natural light and generous views for a most complex set of rooms.

The tower, although stripped of some of its exterior statuary, still maintains its street dominance and contains a spectacular group of rooms. They include a large paneled boardroom at the level of the studio living rooms and a huge, breathtaking octagonal room that occurs at the point where the tower springs free of the rest of the building. The ceiling structure of the tower room is really remarkable as an unusual double truss that is extraordinary for the size and quality of its members.

The contextural specificity of the Chapman Park Studios is remarkable. The continuous hard edge of the building on 6th Street establishes the space of the street in unequivocal terms. The commercial establishments on the sidewalk animate the street and give it its specific character. Finally, the corner tower articulates the place where the building folds to accommodate the side street. In unison with another corner-articulated design across the street (done by the same office), it marks the entrance into Alexandria Street. It provides a palpable physical symbol for the differentiation between the Wilshire business district south of 6th Street and the predominantly residential areas to the north of it.

The Chapman Park Studios are a rare example of the courtyard housing idea applied to a challenging urban site and accommodating a rich mix of activities. The lessons of this kind of building in terms of the potential for urban living in Los Angeles remain unfulfilled.

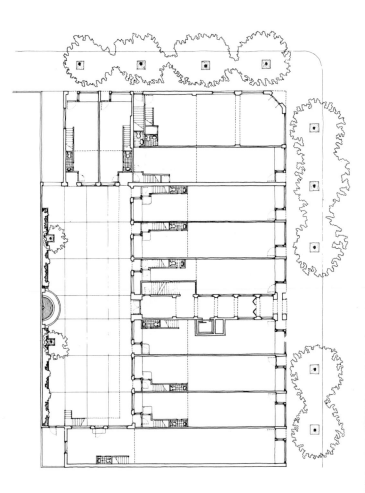

Below, opposite
Chapman Park Studios, 1928,
ground-floor plan.

Below
Chapman Park Studios, 1928, upper
studio plan.

Above right
Chapman Park Studios, 1928, interior
access street.

Below right
Chapman Park Studios, 1928,
entrance into typical studio.

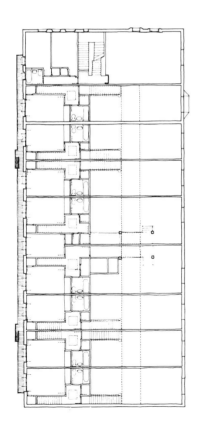

Right
Chapman Park Studios, 1928. The
courtyard has been transformed into
a parking yard.

Below left
Chapman Park Studios, 1928, typical
skylit two-story living room of studio.

Below right
Chapman Park Studios, 1928, ceiling
structure of corner tower.

Right and overleaf
A catalog of the organizational diagrams of all case studies featured in this book drawn to the same scale. Note that the diagrams are ground plan drawings that illustrate the following: relationships to the street, back yard, side yards; relative size and shape of building(s) and courtyard(s); horizontal and vertical circulation. This set of diagrams is not a definitive, closed list of examples of the courtyard housing type; it is rather a collection of the most mature and representative examples of the type observed in Southern California.

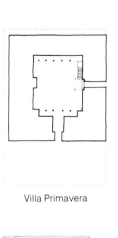

Villa Primavera

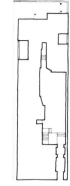

Patio del Moro

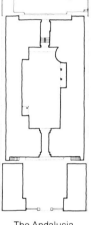

The Andalusia

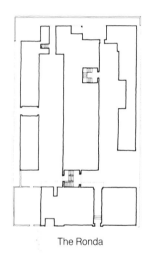

The Ronda

[1]Richard Requa, *Architectural Details: Spain and the Mediterranean* (Los Angeles: Monolith Portland Cement, 1926).
[2]The present owner and soul of the Andalusia for the last four decades, Mrs. Don Uhl, has compiled a partial list of the people who have inhabited this most extraordinary court in the last fifty years: George Allen, CBS executive; Frederick Anthon, restorer of paintings; Stephen Moorehouse Avery, writer; Richard Blake and Eve Green, writers; Claire Bloom, actress; Karl Boehm, actor, son of conductor; Clara Bow, actress; Marlon Brando, Sr., father of actor; Bernice Claire, actress, First National Studios; Emma Dunn, actress; Dorothy Ford, actress; Kenneth Gelman, television actor; Marcos Goshrick, husband of Olivia de Havilland; Jean Hagen, actress; James Hall, musical comedy star, actor, Paramount Studios; Sally Haynes, actress; Peter Hessler, auto racer; Nadrie Hewley, executive, Hughes Productions; Albert Hirschfield, cartoonist; Michael Hogan, writer; John Ireland, actor; Katy Jurado, Mexican actress; Anna Kashfi, actress; Sue Langdon, actress; Martin Kosleck, German actor; Louis L'Amour, writer; Carlo Lastricale, Italian producer; Jeffrey Lazarus, writer; Jay Livingston, songwriter; William Kenneally, CBS Radio newscaster; Cathy Mann, editor, *Teen* magazine; Robert Maxson, performer, Shipstad Ice Follies; Lane McLean, lieutenant commander, U.S. Navy; Edward Paramore, writer; John Payne and Anne Shirley, actors; James Richardson, Paramount Studios; Cesar Romero, actor; Jack Rose, film producer; Harry Rosenthal, concert pianist; Adrian Scott, writer; E. Shipstad, Shipstad Ice Follies; Robert Sinott, artist, muralist; Tracy Swope, television actress; Don Taylor and Phyllis Avery Taylor, actors; Erick von Steinberg, writer; Hans von Twardowsky, German actor; Jay Ward, Ward Productions; Jack Weston, actor; Hamilton Wright, writer; Teresa Wright, actress.
[3]Walter S. Davis et al., *California Garden City Homes: A Book of Stock Plans* (Los Angeles: Garden City Company of California, 1915).

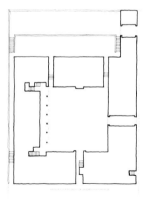

El Cabrillo

Casa Laguna

185

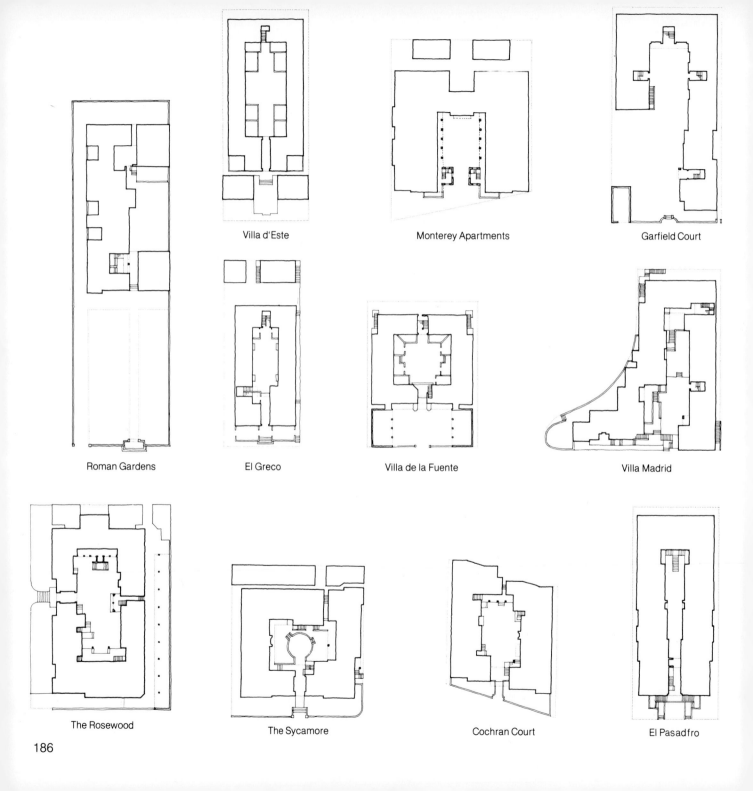

Villa d'Este

Monterey Apartments

Garfield Court

Roman Gardens

El Greco

Villa de la Fuente

Villa Madrid

The Rosewood

The Sycamore

Cochran Court

El Pasadfro

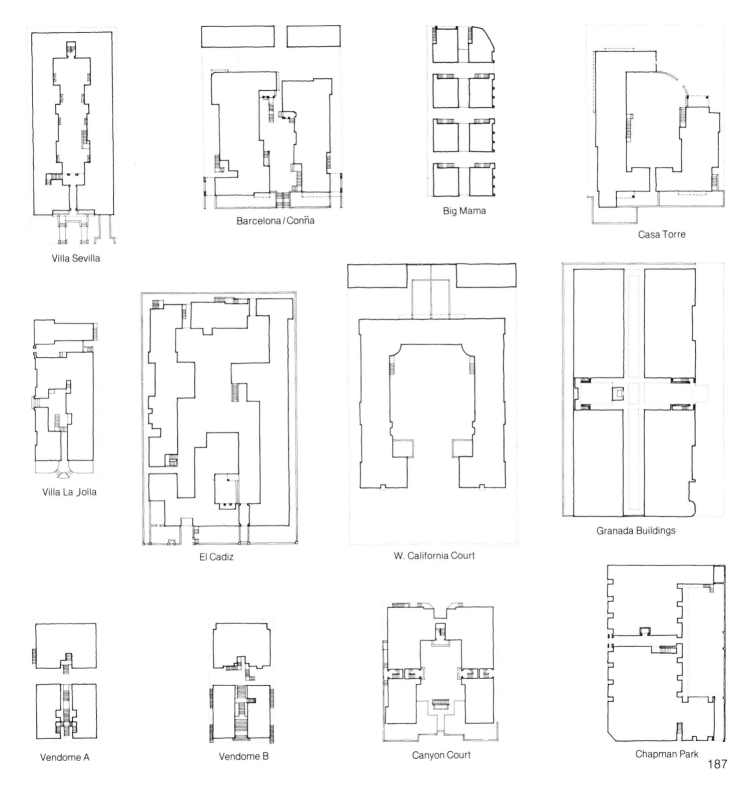

Villa Sevilla

Barcelona / Conña

Big Mama

Casa Torre

Villa La Jolla

El Cadiz

W. California Court

Granada Buildings

Vendome A

Vendome B

Canyon Court

Chapman Park

187

188

Style and Type

6 In every country, the art of correct building is born of a pre-existing source. Everything must have an antecedent; nothing in any genre comes from nothing, and this is applicable to all of man's inventions. Also we see that all things, in depicting later changes, have always conserved their elementary principle making it visible and evident to feeling and reason. It is like a kind of nucleus about which are collected, and consequently to which have been coordinated, the developments and variations of forms to which the object is susceptible. Thus a thousand things have been achieved in each genre; and one of the principal occupations of science and philosophy is to discover the origins and primitive cause in order to understand the reasons. This is what we call *type* in architecture as in every other field of human inventions and institutions.

—Quatremere de Quincy, *Dictionnaire Historique d'Architecture,* 1832

Every substantial architectural tendency carries within it the traces of the method that generated it. Arthur Zwebell's Ronda was being built in Los Angeles at the same time that Le Corbusier's Villa Savoye was being completed in Paris. What are the specific principles that generate two architectural expressions so diametrically opposed to each other?

Perhaps the best means of resolving this question is by reference to objects other than buildings. Le Corbusier's constant allusion to mechanical devices in *Towards a New Architecture* underscored his conviction that their organization and style were necessarily and integrally related. The specific references to the 1921 Delage, the 1921 Voisin, and the 1911 Hispano-Suiza were attempts to illustrate that the development of the form and performance of automobiles could be applied by analogy to buildings. His argument was based on the belief that a programmatic statement of function could generate by careful experiment and selection a standard of perfection; that purpose, operation, and form were definitely developed through application, and not preconception; and that the final synthesis of the three, their ultimate linking, constituted an inevitable and determined cultural act, the climax of human progress.

This thesis became the cornerstone of polemical functionalism in the 1920s and 1930s. It was elaborated in theory and practice by a number of other architects and

Left
Cortijo near Ronda in southern Spain.

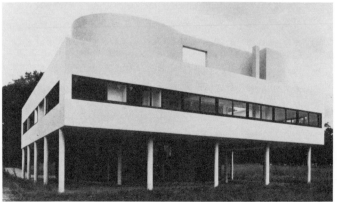

Above and left
Like Villa Savoye, Arthur B. Zwebell's Ronda is the result of a highly rational design process. Unlike Savoye, however, the Ronda's exterior is conceived as a kind of veneer, one that is emotionally separated from the working order of the interior.

Opposite
The capacity to separate exterior from interior is poignantly demonstrated in Zwebell's Bub roadster, a stylized body design for a standard Ford chassis of the 1920s. Unlike Le Corbusier, who viewed the 1921 Delage as an ideal design because of its integration of exterior and interior, Zwebell saw the Bub much as he saw his architecture: a separate outer shell to be applied over an unaffected interior.

has been codified in a variety of Modern Architectural stereotyped slogans: "The exterior is the result of an interior"; "The plan is the generator"; "The 'Styles' are a lie"; "Form follows function"; "Ornament is crime"; and so on.

By contrast, turn-of-the-century eclectic forces were fueled by nostalgia for places and feelings past. In their critical position, their present was viewed as a historical agent incapable of generating form that could express their human uniqueness in time. This stance reflected a necessary acceptance of the machine culture and industrial processes combined with the need to transform the appearance of industrially produced objects.

The disconnection of production from expression, function from style, chassis from body rendered these new industrial-culture objects emotionally accessible and made them capable of being located in the historical continuum of human experience. Arthur Zwebell's 1920 design of a speedster body for Ford cars is formally similar to the 1921 Voisin; but it is paradigmatic of strictly antimodern attitudes. The body is detached from the machinery, and its form is not necessarily connected to that of the industrially developed standard, the legendary Model T Ford.

The promotional brochure for Zwebell's Bub body makes it clear that it is meant to be seen as a styling improvement only. The basic design goals are totally divorced from conceptual or intellectual concerns and address instead the market issues of comfort, pleasure, and status derived from the use of a motor vehicle. The object is presented as a demonstration of the idea that operation and visible form should be happily detached.

The Bub could be used as a departure point for a variety of eclectic counterslogans: "The exterior is independent of an interior"; "The skin is the generator"; "Form follows form"; and so on. Of course, eclecticism was too dominant an attitude to generate polemical statements. Instead it was applied quietly and forcefully as a method and generated some buildings of remarkable quality.

The fundamental theoretical difference between a modern and an eclectic architecture lies in the question of the origin of form. Functionalism rejected all suggestion that historical-formal precedent was of any value whatsoever. As a matter of fact, the application of historical precedent was regarded as a highly decadent act. The educational program of Modern Architecture aimed to purge students of their memories (preconceptions!) and current perceptions in order to prepare them for the development of architectural order ex nuovos through intimate contact with the Zeitgeist. Most of the form produced was abstract, introverted, and defensive. The Bauhaus curriculum, as the model of this kind of training, introduced problems so elementary that their content was limited to learning and production that had only very narrow application to problems of building.

Proponents of eclecticism viewed reference to historical and autonomous architectural ideas as the basis of architectural expression. Its educational program involved exposure to a wide array of formal repertoires and stressed the development of good judgment about the applicability of appropriateness of new stylistic gestures. The resulting architecture was often realistic and theatrical. It invited interpretation by both experience and memory; it was always semantically accessible and reassuring.

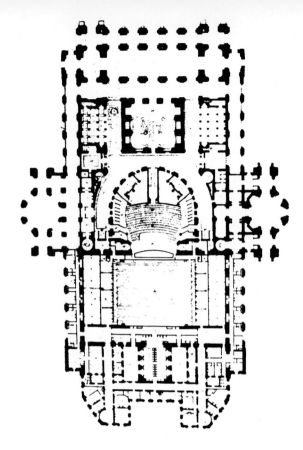

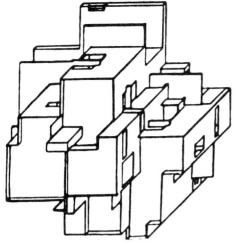

The method of eclecticism at the turn of the century was characterized by a double philosophical and operational dependence: the use of historical stylistic fragments as the foundation of all expression, and their transformation into a whole building through grafting onto the body of historically proven plan/section partis.

In the concrete case of a Los Angeles courtyard housing typology, extraordinary stylistic permutations have been achieved through the combination of diverse historical fragments with typical plan/section partis. The illustrated catalog included here shows only some of the available examples of the application of historic building styles and fragments to existing buildings in southern California.

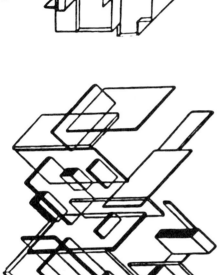

The Modern Movement rejected architectural precedent and attempted the solving of every architectural problem ex nuovo. (Opposite) Tony Garnier, 1853, Paris Opera, plan of amphitheater and dress circle boxes; (left) Theo van Doesburg and Cornelis van Esteren, two studies for a Dwelling House, 1923.

Above left
Egyptian Revival court, Los Angeles,
1920s.

Above right
"Ironic" order court, Los Angeles,
1920s.

Below left
Hansel and Gretel court, Los
Angeles, 1920s.

Above left
Two-story California bungalow court
(remodeled), Hollywood, 1910s.

Above right
Typical classicizing court, Los
Angeles, 1920s.

Below left
Italianate court, Los Angeles, 1920s.

The Spanish Revival was supported—as were the other eclectic tendencies of the nineteenth and twentieth centuries—by particular intellectual and social forces, in this case in southern California. Its proponents saw it as an attitude that was emotionally appropriate in that it accommodated the past but was also contemporary in that it incorporated technical change. The architecture fostered through its stated principles was simultaneously emotionally regressive and thoroughly modern. It is not coincidental that Sheldon Cheney, in his seminal international survey of 1935, *The New World Architecture,* includes a number of "California style" houses as representative of modern design. He clearly saw that the so-called Spanish Revival was developing from a revivalist beginning to increasingly eclectic directions:

Within the decade one has been able to see the phenomenon of hundreds of houses attractively honest and simple, though born of an historic impulse: whittled down to a basic structure and pattern that would appear revolutionary and "new" if we did not recollect the "backward evolutionary" process behind it.

A great many more [houses] illustrate the phenomenon of a Renaissance mode stripped back to elemental massing and rational functioning, with an unmistakable flavour lingering from the original historic source. In general these too (though less significant to us just here) are logical house-machines, with a simple direct beauty that marks them as tolerably of their place and of their time.[1]

The word *revivalism* of course implies the literal repetition of past forms as well as the feelings and circumstances that gave rise to them. The word *eclecticism* describes a less than disciplined practice of combining appropriate historical ingredients to create new overall forms. Both tendencies involve the use of preexisting architectures. Spanish Revival architecture as practiced by the "California style" architects, however, was responsive to context, open to programmatic necessities, and consciously styled to represent the social necessities of its sponsors. Clearly it was not revivalist but mainstream eclectic in spirit. The historical architecture of the Mediterranean region was broken down into a most convenient and meaningful set of formal fragments. These basic elements were detached from their original context and transformed to respond to a new set of local conditions and to create new desired effects.

This process of defining and qualifying a closed set of typical formal ingredients became the stylistic essence of the Spanish Revival. The classical orders were still seen by the Spanish Revival designers as a source of iconographic meaning. Classicism was applied, however, not as a wholesale interpretation of building types, as had been the case with nineteenth-century eclecticism, but rather as a morphology of building elements: an Ionic column here, a composite capital there, a pair of arches in this room, a classical balustrade on that balcony, a dentil range in wood along that fascia. The orders were used purely as picturesque fragments, a kind of antiquarian veneer applied to buildings derived from other ideas and sources.

Eclecticism in southern California courts focused on the definition of semantic fragments at a scale larger than that of the elements of the classical orders. The formulation of categories of such eclectic compositional and building blocks was based on their ability to communicate. Fragments were typified as carriers of meaning that could evoke particular emotions. They were organized as a kit of parts that reflected most, if not all, kinesthetic experiences in architecture: doors represented passage; fireplaces symbolized warmth and security; windows reflected the possibility of access to light and view; balconies and balustrades suggested the possibility of extension beyond the body of the building. Style was seen as emanating from all that was visible and interpretable in architecture. For that reason alone, it developed into an issue that could be resolved only in section and elevation. Thus the formal properties of building as machine were detached from building as image.

Eclecticism marked a definite swing away from conceptual design. Architecture was thought of as a narrative describing particular human conditions or experiences. The stylistic origin of any one fragment utilized was not related to its authenticity or pedigree. Instead, it had to belong to an identifiable typology of stylistic elements and had to be used consistently to create the desired picturesque effects.

A typology of stylistic fragments superimposed on a typology of plan/section organizations gave rise to eclectic architectures that were disciplined, predictable, and at the same time highly expressive. The genius of the Spanish Revival lies in part in the seeming contradiction of tremendous

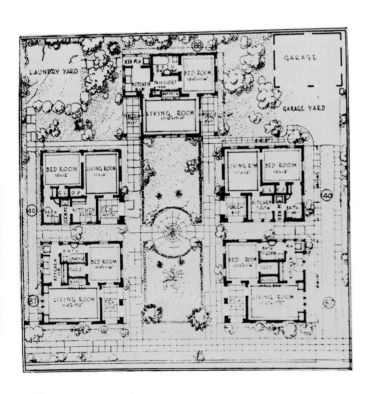

Below
A stair from the Ronda copied from
an illustration of Quinta de Arrizafa in
Cordova, from the Bynes' *Spanish
Gardens and Patios*. Such pattern
books were stock references in the
offices of southern California
architects.

stylistic diversity arising out of strict, visible principles of organization.

The syntactic rules of combination of Spanish Revival fragments fall within three categories. First, the literal revivalist transference of images from the southern Spanish prototypes to southern California buildings reproduced accurately the formal qualities of the original. Second, in many instances fragments were assembled by conventional references and reflected particular conditions within a building. Examples of this type of usage are the local symmetries in parts of elevations of Zwebell's Ronda and the typical picturesque juxtapositions of windows and doors used to create overall asymmetry in such buildings as Zwebell's Patio del Moro. Finally, the most elaborate and ambitious attempts to generate richness of expression occur with buildings in which fragments are combined in unique and often contradictory ways. The multiple scalar references of the Granada Buildings and the Villa Madrid indicate the achievement of formal coherence through novel syntactical means. This is clearly the highest level of eclectic accomplishment.

Right
This is another example of literal copying. The tile-embellished, double-arched balcony window in Old Cordoba published in the Bynes' *Spanish Gardens and Patios* reappears in Arthur B. Zwebell's Andalusia of 1926. This very popular motif is found in many other Los Angeles courts.

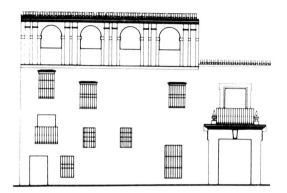

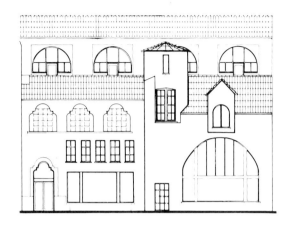

Above and below
The overall composition of Zwebell's Ronda is not a literal copy of a specific building. It shares, however, a common set of architectural elements (e.g., windows, doors, moldings) and certainly captures the stylistic flavor of many Spanish prototypes, including this example from Seville.

Above
The Granada Buildings are a repository of architectural quotes from every conceivable Spanish source, but ingeniously collaged into a structure that is simultaneously Spanish and distinctly rational and Modern.

The actual method of Spanish Revival design was supported by the publication of elaborate manuals. Some were published by trade organizations, tile companies, plaster companies, and so on, while others were published by architectural scholars. The former supported an unabashed pictorial preference for revivalist form and advertised the material possibilities for making it happen. The latter placed eclecticism in general, and the Spanish Revival in particular, in its cultural context. They provided most of the elaborate and historically important explanations for the development of eclectic tendencies.

The trade books were published locally, while the intellectual defenses of eclecticism were sponsored on the East Coast. Every architect's office was well stocked with such volumes, many of which were offered for sale through architectural magazines. Old architects' offices that are still in operation and architectural libraries in the Los Angeles region are full of these documents. At the University of Southern California Library, one such donated treatise belonged to the Pasadena architect Edward Babcock. The year of acquisition of the book is 1926, and the date appears under the architect's signature. One year after he bought the book, Babcock designed one of the elaborate Spanish Revival courts on East California Boulevard in Pasadena.

The actual mechanics of the process of design in a "Spanish style" centered on the act of translating perspectives, photographs, and occasional measured drawings into plans, sections, and elevations appropriate to the design tasks at hand. Harold Bissner, Sr., codesigner with Arthur Zwebell of El Cabrillo Court in Hollywood, described the process in a recent interview: "The book was all photographs, single plates like these. You could take them out, put them on your drafting board, and say 'Now, I'm going to do that mantel . . . reproduce that mantel . . . I see in front of me, or that doorway.' That was the nature of that thing. Details!! . . . Put all your details together, and pretty soon you have a nice house. That's the way Spanish houses were designed, in my estimation. I don't think Americans were original in that aspect at all."

Above
A pastoral Andalusian scene from *The Minor Ecclesiastical, Domestic, and Garden Architecture of Southern Spain* by Austin Whittlesey. Architects in southern California were well aware of books like this.

Right
Photographs from still other books, such as this illustration from *Spanish Gardens and Patios* by Arthur and Mildred Stapley Byne, were provocative references to the imagined Spanish roots of southern California.

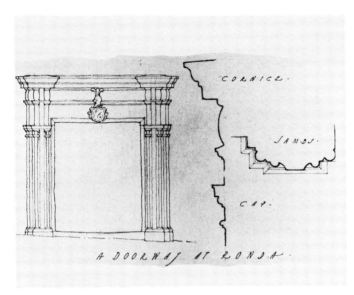

CORNICE.

JAMBS.

CAP.

A DOORWAY AT RONDA.

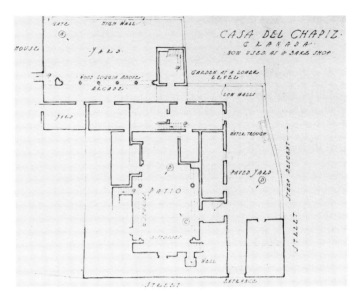

CASA DEL CHAPIZ.
GRANADA.
NOW USED AS A BAKE SHOP.

Above left
These trade books included not only sketches of building scenes but details of fragments of buildings such as windows and doorways, as in this example from Whittlesey, "A doorway at Ronda."

Above right
Spanish patio buildings, such as this portion of the Casa del Chapiz from Whittlesey, provided convenient and tantalizing models.

203

As an homage to eclectic practice at the turn of the century, we include here an illustrated catalog of formal fragments based on Richard Requa's book, *Architectural Details: Spain and the Mediterranean,* published by the Monolith Portland Cement Company in 1926.[2]

The enumeration and hierarchical ordering of the fragments as exhibited below clearly express the vocabulary and stylistic priorities of the Spanish Revival:

1. Street scenes and general views
2. Buildings, country type
3. Buildings, city type
4. Roofs, towers, cornices, chimneys
5. Doorways
6. Window grills
7. Balconies and balustrades
8. Courts and patios
9. Garden details
10. Stairs, ceilings, fireplaces
11. Fountains, floors, walls, gates
12. Ornamented ironwork

These details illustrate the wide
variety of Spanish Revival fragments
used to embellish the courts.

These details illustrate the wide variety of Spanish Revival fragments used to embellish the courts.

A new regional building technology that evolved in the first decade of this century contributed significantly to the realization of the white stucco, tile-roofed buildings that were the icons of the Spanish Revival. Originally, of course, adobe was the natural indigenous building material. With no forests close at hand, an adobe-block building covered with a pole frame and handmade tile roof was a logical type of structure to build, and the ranchos and missions were made exactly this way. Sometimes the adobe block was covered with a coat of stucco or clay but was more typically, as with the ranchos, left as unfinished adobe. Adobe masonry structures, however, are especially vulnerable to the lateral loads imposed by earthquakes. The known history of building collapse and the anticipation of future earthquakes must have made builders wary of adobe construction.

The availability of lumber made possible by the development of port facilities at San Pedro and the expansion of the railroads gave another alternative to masonry construction, and adobe was rapidly replaced by western framing as the dominant residential construction technology. It took another invention, though, to make wooden building the suitable vehicle for much of the Spanish Revival architecture.

Plaster stucco was typically applied to masonry buildings of adobe, brick, or clay tile. Since moisture penetrates stucco, a problem of adhesion between the stucco and the masonry structure always persisted. Even where rainfall was light, moisture penetration on a wooden frame was a problem. A wooden building could logically be covered with wood, however, and be simply painted. Most of the earlier houses of Los Angeles were, indeed, the wooden mimes of their East Coast and northern California prototypes. Although quite resistant to earthquake stressing, wooden buildings that were painted did not hold up well and gave little protection from intense summer sun. Someone thought of covering the wood frame with tar paper for moisture protection and a layer of chicken wire for strength and adhesion. Now stucco (later to be called Gunite, when it could be pumped through a nozzle) could be easily, effectively, and cheaply applied to wood-frame buildings. It was waterproof, could withstand the harsh effects of direct sunlight, and was resistant to termites and earthquakes. To apply stucco to chicken wire was, in effect, like putting a one-inch reinforced shell around a wooden frame. In the event of an earthquake, cracks were easily repaired. The quake-resistant properties of wire-reinforced stucco were widely advertised; in fact, the Gunite trademark included the phrase "Gunite, quake-resisting reinforced Veneer."

Significantly, this building technology lent itself admirably to the duplication of stucco prototypes, whether they were local or exotic. Their style could now be easily and cheaply reproduced, and the pursuit of a Spanish Revival architecture mushroomed, carried, literally, on the strength of a simple and ingenious invention.

The production support available from various manufacturers, assemblers, distributors, and contractors was largely responsible for the quality execution of the architectural intentions of southern California's eclectic architects up to 1930. Companies and individuals were not only connected to the mainstream of the ancient crafts but were also well versed in the productive possibilities of the machine. Relatively low labor wages allowed for much custom design at a time when eclectic designers proposed the relearning of long-forgotten or new formal sensibilities.

Typically, a deluxe Spanish Revival court was built by a combination of modern and ancient trades. The *Pasadena Star-News* shows the following specialists collaborating in the construction of the West California Court:[3]

John Simpson, General Contractor
Jones Electric Co.
Orban Lumber Co.
Walter Speer, Plumber
Pasadena Roofing Co.
Alhambra Kilns Inc., Roof and Floor Tile
Crown City Nurseries
Southern California Hardwood and Manufacturing Co.
Pasadena Sheet Metal Works, Heating
Calloway Tile and Marble Co., Decorative Tile
Stockton and Spurgin Inc., Hardware and Supplies
John Sympson, Painting and Decorating
Bernarr Judson Garrett, Wrought Iron
Dependable Window Shade and Awning Co.
'Servel' Electric Refrigeration
Overhead Door Co.

The coming of the depression in 1929 changed both the intellectual and the material basis for eclectic design. Faith in a defunct past was replaced by faith in an illusory modern future; and the tentative balance of construction wages, price of materials, and client incomes was replaced by new economic formulas that excluded in a terminal sense quality products.

Above
The manufacturers of Gunite were well aware of the strength and durability of reinforced stucco.

[1]Sheldon Cheney, *The New World Architecture* (New York: Tudor Publishing, 1935), pp. 268–72.
[2]Richard Requa, *Architectural Details: Spain and the Mediterranean* (Los Angeles: Monolith Portland Cement, 1926), pt. 1, p. 7.
[3]*Pasadena Star-News*, June 9, 1928.

Epilogue
The Lessons of the Courts

Human beings gain a sense of identity and orientation by reference to particular urban pieces, buildings, or landscapes. Landmarks are used as a means of extracting uniqueness of place within an otherwise undifferentiated urban fabric; they fulfill the need to supply the city with physical attributes of memory and tradition.

Because they communicate to us some measure of the achievement of the societies that built them, landmarks also serve as reminders of our responsibilities and as challenges to our own sensibilities. In this sense, there exists an obvious need to protect and conserve some of the fabulous courts that we have described. Conservation efforts should focus first on the declaration of these buildings as landmarks. Further, they should be protected both from wanton destruction by development and from insidious destruction through unsympathetic redesign and lack of proper maintenance. These protected courts will challenge us to define new buildings that match their qualities of place, their high standards of construction, and their suggestions of the possibility of a full and serene life in the city.

Most of Los Angeles was laid out along the agricultural property line and road pattern established by the Continental Survey. Consequently, the basic component of the urban pattern that emerged was the square grid with major intersections every mile. The edges of these mile-square sections are ringed by commercial avenues that typically enclose single-family house precincts.

Sometimes, additional streets within each section become smaller commercial strips or support higher-density residential development. From the first decade of the century on, such clusters of residential hotels, apartments, or duplexes were established within the mile-by-mile quasi superblock, often in proximity to major boulevards, such as Sunset or Wilshire. Most examples of courtyard housing examined in this study are now scattered about these urban high-density pockets. Most apartment construction of recent years has occurred in attempts to enlarge and increase the density of these areas. Very few of the new buildings, however, have been able to achieve the exceptional qualities and contextual responsiveness of the older courtyard buildings.

Above
Several of the finest courtyard
buildings in Los Angeles are
concentrated in this area of West
Hollywood south of Sunset
Boulevard between Harper and
Havenhurst. The entrance to Villa
d'Este can be seen in the upper right
portion of this photo, as can several
other of the deluxe courts. The
comparison between the old and the
new apartment buildings is quite
striking.

To a certain extent this is due to the fact that Los Angeles is a severely discontinuous city. It is often difficult for architects to interpret what the elements of urban order are at any given site so that they can be taken into account. Worse still, architects tend to constrain their concerns and formal consciousness to the boundaries of the single site. By and large, those who design, finance, and build housing do not possess the awareness that their buildings are the means by which the city is constructed, that from their separate actions there results an aggregate form that is real and long lasting.

By contrast with the current situation of virtual contextual anarchy, the courtyard-housing typology as built in Los Angeles in the period 1900–1930 can be a valuable model of how we should proceed in restructuring our cities. These buildings exemplify the crucial order and collective structure that our urban design efforts currently lack.

It is perhaps high time that preservationist efforts begin to shift their focus away from the obsession of saving single buildings and toward the breathing of new life into urban districts of unusual quality. The value of these districts should be determined not only by the concentration of individually distinguished buildings within them but also by the capability of all buildings, new and old, landmarks and simple fillers, to generate a city form of distinction.

A prerequisite of district-scale preservation should be that buildings share common, identifiable urban qualities. These include the contextual attributes of buildings, such as their relationship to the ground plane, their ability to form special configurations (arcades, passages, terraces), their ability to define and enclose urban spaces (alleys, streets, avenues, boulevards, squares), or the variety of openings, materials, and colors that constitute their facades.

The typological consistency of buildings is largely responsible for the quality of the resulting urban form. If one accepts this premise, two very serious consequences arise. First, there is no serious divergence of goals or methods between preservation and urban design. The value of buildings lies in their capacity as "building blocks" to generate the city and the life that is acted out within it. In the process of urban change, the sense of order in any given district has to be established in order to guide its future development. Distinguished as well as modest buildings can be vital in their role

as carriers of that sense of order. For instance, in the case of Los Angeles courtyard housing, widely accepted building types were applied in stylistically diverse but typologically continuous ways and generated beautiful city fragments. The act of saving older buildings could also formally guide the restructuring of the city.

Second, urban planning as has been practiced and made bureaucratic in the last thirty years places a low priority on the quality of the city as a place. This kind of planning is largely verbal and consequently nonformal. Extraordinary decisions about urban form are being made every day in this country without reference to their physical consequences. Two-dimensional zoning, density increases in given areas, prescriptive standards, superimposition of new rapid transit systems on existing cities, location of new institutions—all are being applied without any consideration of their effects on the existing typological and physical structure of the city or the ability of the individual buildings to generate the overall form of the city. Examples of the complete destruction of cities by the imposition of typologically discontinuous buildings abound. The time has come to stress a fact that is almost self-evident: that new buildings conceived in a vacuum are not capable of creating a city. Large-scale planning without a stress on typological continuity and morphological consistency becomes an agent of unchecked private economic interests at best or a generator of organized chaos—a product typical of the bureaucratic postindustrial state—at worst.

If a small minority of courts should be preserved for all their assorted virtues as isolated monuments, the overwhelming majority of them should be taken into account for their ability to shape our cities by providing meaningful buildings and places within it. Their typological structure should be interpreted and adhered to, and the understanding of courts as type should lead to the extensive study of other building types, so that the complete structure of the city can become uncovered, understood, and useful as a guide for future development.

It is inevitable that there will continue to be an increase in the amount of housing construction in multifamily configurations in the United States. In the last twenty-five years, the cost of housing has increased at over twice the rate of family income. The result of this trend has been a steady erosion of the middle-income family's homeowning capability; one family in three could afford to buy a home in 1966 (assuming the Department of Housing and Urban Development standard of paying no more than four times annual income for a house), but only one out of ten can afford to today. While there is a current preference for single-family houses in southern California, it is probable that apartments and other forms of dense urban housing will continue to be built at a rate that will rapidly overtake the rate of single-family home construction.

The typical bland Los Angeles apartment building does not offer an attractive housing choice in a region where an extravagant form of suburban housing has long flourished. If apartment living for families is to be a viable alternative to the single-family house, it must offer some of the presumed amenities of suburban living: quiet, privacy, security, adequate outdoor space, easy accommodation of the automobile, and the miscellaneous equipment of today's recreation-oriented family.

If we can expect a denser form of living accommodations in the future, it is certainly a worthwhile undertaking to identify as well as document the salient characteristics of significant existing housing types. It is equally important to apply the lessons of the courts at the scale of the single building to future housing efforts. How have new buildings failed to incorporate the typological logic of the older buildings? Why has urban discontinuity become a typical feature of so much new housing? What new strategies can we pursue in order to return to a tradition of housing where the individual building is a vital link to a larger urban network?

There are many and complex answers to these questions, but they are generally attributable to a few factors that range from current building practices, code restrictions, and market assumptions to an apparent failure to recognize and apply the typological lessons of existing buildings.

The basic construction technology of housing has changed little in the last sixty years; wood-frame construction with a stucco exterior skin is still the norm. The increase in the price of capital, labor, and materials, however, and the catastrophic collapse of the quality of the craft of building have generated housing forms that are shallow, opportunistic constructions, a response to quantitative factors only.

Below
Entrance facade of a typical Los Angeles low-rise, high-density courtyard apartment building constructed in the 1950s.

Much recent housing is typologically destructive because it does not address even the elementary issues of architecture. In many recent instances, construction technology has come to replace architecture. The result is confusion in all respects, including a sacrifice in the quality of living place, the imagery of housing forms, or the form of the city as a whole.

Codes have changed radically since the 1920s, and they are the greatest evident factor for the abandonment of many desirable courtyard housing features. Profound changes have occurred as a result of the adoption of rigorous fireproof-construction, exit, and parking requirements.

The courtyard form of apartment building still prevails in Los Angeles where sites are large enough to allow generous open space. At first glance, a typical courtyard apartment building of today looks similar to the older buildings: a building that fronts the street, two or three stories high, surrounding and presumably opening upon a courtyard garden. Upon closer inspection, however, one realizes that there have been subtle but profound modifications of the idea. The parking garages that are so discreetly handled in the originals through the use of a lovely tiled forecourt off the street, a small entrance from a small garage on the rear alley, or even an underground arrangement have now been replaced by a massive concrete garage below grade but open on the side to prevent the necessity for the forced ventilation that would otherwise be required. Not only is the garage now a highly visible sea of cars, but entrance to the buildings is up half a level from the street, an accommodation to the space of the garage. The pleasant vestibule space at the grade off the sidewalk which one finds in buildings like Villa d'Este and the Andalusia is now impossible, and entrance from the sidewalk is typically unresolved. Attempts to disguise the problem with monumental stairs and elaborate plantings only draw further attention to the fact that the garage problem is seldom satisfactorily solved. The street is not the only element given over to the auto; much of the sidewalk and the entrance to the building are as well.

Perhaps we overaccommodate the automobile today, and one wonders if the parking requirements are really reasonable when they impinge so much on the quality of life outside the car. The early courtyard apartments had off-street parking too, but they were not as rigid about it as apartment

buildings are today. Cars are parked in tandem at the Villa d'Este—an inconvenience, to be sure, but the residents manage, and there is a great savings in space.

Programs aimed at reducing the negative impact of parking restrictions upon housing design should begin with an acknowledgment that parking standards need not be absolute but should be variable and should take into account, among other things, topography, amount of land capable of being built on, and number of units to be provided. Cities could put into effect bonus plans where, for example, a builder could be allowed to build higher than normally permitted if the garage were completely below grade with forced ventilation. Reducing the parking-per-unit requirements (will there always be so many cars?), parking small cars together, tandem parking, and creating spaces for bicycles and motorcycles are all provisions that reduce the total space allocated to the automobile.

No strategy concerning parking should be formulated without an examination of the formal effects of what is otherwise a set of verbal prescriptions that impact heavily upon the shape of buildings and the city and therefore upon people's ways of life. Most, if not all, courts illustrated in this book are rendered obsolete by current zoning regulations with reference to parking.

A closer inspection of a typical new courtyard apartment building reveals other subtle departures from its older counterparts. The simple garden with pleasant fountain, beautiful foliage and flowers—a quiet, private space that frequently serves as the extension of interior space—has been replaced, usually by a swimming pool. While a pool is itself an attractive idea in a mild climate, it radically changes the garden ambiance of the courtyard. Instead of being the exterior extension of private interior space, a place for introspection, the courtyard becomes a highly public space devoted to recreation. The nature of the traditional court type is thus completely compromised.

Entrance and circulation in new buildings differ dramatically from the same elements in the older prototypes. Entrance to the individual apartments in the older courts is directly from the courtyard either by individual doors or by small stairs to the upper levels, with each stair providing entry to several apartments. Sometimes, as in the Villa d'Este, for example,

Left
Access corridor of a typical 1950s
courtyard apartment building. The
open corridors that ring the
courtyard destroy its sense of
tranquility and enclosure. The living
rooms that open onto the corridor
lose their sense of privacy. Minimum
construction masquerading as
architecture robs the whole building
of any sense of style or place.

Below left
The courtyard of a typical 1950s
courtyard apartment building. The
center is occupied by a swimming
pool. The walls are eroded by public
corridors, the architecture is
reduced to mere minimum
construction. The magic is gone!

small, walled-in patios are formed within the larger space of the garden. Entrance here is through the small, private garden space, which also doubles as exterior space for living and dining. While the stairs are usually contained within the overall building form, sometimes they become interesting objects in this space, as do the stairs of the Rosewood, for instance, where one ascends in the garden area to small access balconies overlooking the garden from above. In all of these buildings, however, entrance is discreet and pleasant, and intraunit circulation is internal. Most also have separate service access on the sides.

Requirements for multiple fire exits and a reluctance to build maisonette-type apartments have made a corridor or gallery type of access to all upper units practically mandatory. Instead of private entrances handled in such a manner that interior spaces open directly to exterior gardens, the courtyard is now ringed with the public access gallery at each floor. This not only contradicts the basic idea of the building—apartments that look inward upon a garden—but also seriously reduces the quality of privacy in the courtyard. Furthermore, most apartments turn their backs on the garden and open instead to the space between buildings or to the street.

It would seem logical to put the access gallery on the exterior of the building, between buildings, so that private spaces—living rooms, dining rooms, bedrooms—could open to the garden, but fire codes again make this economically unviable. The open gallery is allowed on the garden but must be enclosed and fire rated (with fire doors, limited openings, and wire glass) if it extends more than one-third of the distance to the property line. In other words, the only way that the open corridor could be used on the outside of the building would be either to turn it into a fire-rated corridor or to reduce the allowable volume of the building—both unattractive options to a builder trying to maximize his or her investment. The result is garden gallery corridors on the upper floors of most recent apartment buildings that use the courtyard idea.

Again, a bonus system applicable if either exterior corridors or multiple stairs were used to meet access-egress requirements might be applied as an incentive to induce builders to make more intelligent use of the courtyards. Other alternatives, such as fire escapes and changes in the code to allow exit via connecting balconies through an adjacent apartment, might also be explored.

The maisonette apartment, sometimes with a two-story-high living room and with bedrooms and bath above, was very popular in the older courts. While few builders are willing to "waste" the space of even a small double-volume room, these apartments are beautiful and desirable. The maisonette also offers an egress advantage: no upper multiple fire exit is required, so there could be a savings in total cost, at least for a two-story building.

There exists the obvious temptation to search for reasons for the demise of courtyard housing in Los Angeles in pragmatic and deterministic extrinsic factors, such as those outlined above. Perhaps the most fundamental reason for the loss of our building traditions, however, lies in the qualitative transformations that our culture has been subjected to in the last fifty years.

What has transpired in the United States since the depression is a break in the necessary relationship between people and buildings. The objects that we generate are not meant to mark the passage of time and to define meaningful spaces. Buildings are not intended to celebrate our brief and tentative lives. Instead they have been transformed into instruments of economic utility. The effects of this change on architecture and urban design have been profound.

The most important fact of the current condition of architecture is the sense of a loss of faith in a future that can be affected, even perhaps improved, through our collective efforts in building. The loss of the dream has changed the perception of whole communities about the nature of their being. In southern California, the dream of generating an oasis of order within a literal and metaphorical desert was a predominant vision in the 1910s and 1920s. It informed both the organizational and the stylistic aspects of architecture. It has been replaced by the inert process of coping. With few exceptions, all the actors involved with the drama of design and building have substituted the ethic and aesthetic of survival for their traditional orientation of responsibility to a future worth living in and for.

The housing shortage in Los Angeles is of such high proportions that citizens are experiencing a constant need to establish basic places to live despite the spatial or material quality of these places. Sponsors of housing, who are generally insensitive to the cultural history and aspirations of the southern California region, have to deal with a bureaucracy that almost a priori transforms the labor of their efforts into a commodity. The issues that they focus on are limited in scope and overwhelmingly quantitative and abstract (sizes, amounts, returns, and the like).

Architects and builders in turn serve the basic orientations of their sponsors. The majority of them are neither contextually inclined nor sensitive to the culture of their city. Most local architectural traditions have expired. Responsible academic eclecticism and the rationalism of the modern pioneers have both given way to confused stylistic tendencies that defy categorization. Somehow the process of generating a building has become more important than the building itself. The remedies necessary to digest and use the lessons of courtyard housing in Los Angeles are difficult to pose in the state of cultural flux that currently prevails.

Perhaps the greatest responsibility for interjecting new ideas into housing falls on the shoulders of architects, who have to reactivate what has always been the hidden agenda of their profession beyond serving the narrow interests of single clients. It is architects who have to help establish the nature of the order of existing cities and aim to incorporate it in their work. It is architects who have to return architecture to the task of making places and objects meaningful to the lives and thoughts and feelings of people. It is architects who should spearhead the fight to change all the destructive rules and conventions that stand in the way of architecture.

It is only when the dreams of the inhabitants of housing align with the energies and critical sense of architects that housing typologies will be respected and extended, and courts may begin to appear again.

A typical terraced Court scene in the
semi-tropical landscape of Echo Park
Lake only a few minutes from downtown Los Angeles.

Bibliography

Bailley, Vernon Howe. *Little Known Towns of Spain*. New York: William Helburn, 1927.

Byne, Arthur. *Spanish Ironwork*. New York: Hispanic Society of America, 1915.

———. *Decorated Wooden Ceilings in Spain*. New York: G. P. Putnam's Sons, 1920.

———. *Spanish Interiors and Furniture*. New York: William Helburn, 1921.

Byne, Arthur, and Mildred Stapley. *Spanish Architecture of the Sixteenth Century*. New York: G. P. Putnam's Sons, 1917.

———. *Spanish Gardens and Patios: Philadelphia and London*. New York: J. B. Lippincott, Architectural Record, 1924.

———. *Provincial Houses in Spain*. New York: William Helburn, 1927.

———. *Majorcan Houses and Gardens*. New York: William Helburn, 1928.

Bottomley, William Lawrence. *Spanish Details*. New York: Brentano's, 1925.

Casa Valdes, Marquesa de. *Jardines de España*. Madrid: Aguilar Ediciones, 1973.

Collantes de Teran Delorme, Francisco, and Luis Gomez Estern. *Arquitectura Civil Sevillana*. Seville: Ayuntamiento de Sevilla, 1976.

Davis, Walter S., et al. *California Garden City Homes: A Book of Stock Plans*. Los Angeles: Garden City Company of California, 1915. Rev. ed. 1916 as *Ideal Homes in Garden Communities: A Book of House Plans*.

Eberlein, H. D. *Villas of Florence and Tuscany*. Philadelphia: J. B. Lippincott, 1922.

Feduchi, Luis. *Arquitectura Popular Española*. Vol. 4. Barcelona: Los Pueblos Blancos, Editorial Blume, 1978.

Fernandez Arenas, Jose. *Mozarabic Architecture*. Greenwich, Conn.: New York Graphic Society, 1972.

Flores, Carlos. *Arquitectura Popular Española*. Madrid: Aguilar Ediciones, 1973.

Galotti, Jean. *Le Jardin et la Maison Arabes du Maroc*. Vols. 1 and 2. Paris: Editions Albert Levy, 1926.

Garcia y Bellido Antonio, et al. *Resumen Historico del Urbanismo en España*. Madrid: Instituto de Estudios de Administracion Local, 1968.

Garcia de Cortaza, G. A. *La España Medieval*. Historia de España Alfaguarra, vol. 2. Madrid: Alianza Editorial, 1976.

Garrison, Richard, and George Rustay. *Mexican Houses*. New York: Architectural Book Publishing, 1930.

Gebhart, David. "Spanish Colonial Revival in Southern California (1895–1930)." *Journal of the Society of Architectural Historians*, May 1967.

Gebhart, David, and Robert Winter. *A Guide to Architecture in Los Angeles and Southern California*. Salt Lake City: Peregrine-Smith, 1977.

Geist, Carl Friederich. *Passagen*. Munich: Prestel-Verlag, 1969.

Goodhue, Bertram. *A Book of Architectural and Decorative Drawings*. New York: Architectural Book Publishing, 1914.

Hannaford, Donald, and Revel Edwards. *Spanish Colonial and Adobe Architecture of California, 1800–1850*. New York: Architectural Book Publishing, 1931.

Hielscher, Kurt. *Picturesque Spain*. New York: Brentano's, 1928.

Irving, Washington. *Tales of the Alhambra*. Granada: Editorial Miguel Sanchez, 1977.

Kirker, Harold. *California's Architectural Frontier*. San Marino, Calif.: Huntington Library, 1970.

Lowell, Guy. *Smaller Italian Villas and Farmhouses*. Vols. 1 and 2. New York: Architectural Book Publishing, 1922.

Mack, Gerstle, and Thomas Gibson. *Architectural Details of Northern and Central Spain*. New York: William Helburn, 1928.

——. *Architectural Details of Southern Spain*. New York: William Helburn, 1928.

Mayer, August. *Architecture and Applied Arts of Old Spain*. New York: Brentano's, 1921.

McWilliams, Carey. *Southern California: An Island on the Land*. Salt Lake City: Peregrine-Smith, 1973.

Morgenthau Fox, Helen. *Patio Gardens*. New York: Macmillan, 1929.

Newcomb, Rexford. *Mediterranean Domestic Architecture in the United States*. Cleveland: J. H. Hansen, 1928.

Polley, G. H. *Spanish Architecture and Ornament*. New York: G. H. Polley, 1889.

Prieto-Moreno, Francisco. *Los Jardines de Granada*. Madrid: Direccion General de Bellas Artes, Ministerio de Educacion y Ciencia, 1973.

Requa, Richard. *Architectural Details: Spain and the Mediterranean*. Los Angeles: Monolith Portland Cement, 1926.

——. *Old World Inspiration for American Architecture*. Los Angeles: Monolith Portland Cement, 1929.

Sexton, R. W. *Spanish Influence on American Architecture and Decoration*. New York: Brentano's, 1928.

Soule, Winsor. *Spanish Farm Houses and Minor Public Buildings*. With an introduction by Ralph Adams Cram. New York: Architectural Book Publishing, 1923.

Standish-Nichols, Rose. *Spanish and Portuguese Gardens*. Boston and New York: Houghton Mifflin, 1924.

Stanton, J. E. *By Middle Seas*. Los Angeles: Gladding, McBean, 1927.

Van Pelt, Garrett. *Old Architecture of Southern Mexico*. Cleveland: J. H. Jansen, 1926.

Weerheijm, Tom, et al. *Hofjes in Nederland*. Haarlem: J. H. Gottmer, 1977.

Whittlesey, Austin. *The Minor Ecclesiastical, Domestic, and Garden Architecture of Southern Spain*. With a preface by Bertram Goodhue. New York: Architectural Book Publishing, 1923.

——. *The Renaissance Architecture of Central and Northern Spain*. New York: Architectural Book Publishing, 1920.

Yerbury, F. B. *Lesser Known Architecture of Spain*. New York: William Helburn, 1926.

Index